Denkart Europa

Schriften zur europäischen Politik, Wirtschaft und Kultur | 25

The series is edited by ASKO EUROPA-STIFTUNG, Saarbrücken and Europäische Akademie Otzenhausen gGmbH.

Tony Venables

Piecing together Europe's Citizenship

Searching for Cinderella

 **Nomos**

© Coverpicture: fotolia.com

The Deutsche Nationalbibliothek lists this publication in the
Deutsche Nationalbibliografie; detailed bibliographic data
are available on the Internet at http://dnb.d-nb.de

ISBN   978-3-8487-3113-8 (Print)
         978-3-8452-7483-6 (ePDF)

British Library Cataloguing-in-Publication Data
A catalogue record for this book is available from the British Library.

ISBN   978-3-8487-3113-8 (Print)
         978-3-8452-7483-6 (ePDF)

Library of Congress Cataloging-in-Publication Data
Venables, Tony
Piecing together Europe's Citizenship
Searching for Cinderella
Tony Venables
193 p.
Includes bibliographic references.

ISBN   978-3-8487-3113-8 (Print)
         978-3-8452-7483-6 (ePDF)

1. Edition 2016
© Nomos Verlagsgesellschaft, Baden-Baden, Germany 2016. Printed and bound in Germany.

PREFACE
Citizens' Rights, Involvement and Trust

This book attempts to fill a gap where European citizenship should be. There are different communities of interest defending European citizens' rights, attempting to reform the European Union so that citizens participate in more critical mass or who organise educational exchanges to build bridges across populations of 28 European countries. In one way or another, this is all about European citizenship, but where and what is it exactly? Something is missing despite the increasingly frequent use of the term *"European citizen"* in a wide variety of contexts. The different communities of interest rarely converge. As a result a wide range of meanings is attached to European citizenship.

In 2013, the European Institutions celebrated the 20th anniversary of the inclusion of Union citizenship in the EU Treaties at Maastricht. This took the form of a special "year", but it was not called the year of European Citizenship. That would have been too difficult, too controversial and no one would have known what it meant. Instead it became a vague "European Year of Citizens". This resulted in awareness raising about European rights and a general debate on the future of Europe, without clear focus. The year was extended to 2014, but this did not bring further clarification.

In order to search for the answers to the question, what is European citizenship, I approached the Rowntree Charitable Trust which generously provided a grant towards this book. Lack of time whilst I was working for ECAS (European Citizen Action Service) and the pressure of immediate deadlines always resulted in yet another postponement. In reality, whilst practical experience was an advantage, it was a difficult book to write before I left ECAS at the end of 2013 and had more time. In the course of researching for this book, European citizenship was confronted – and largely failed – a number of "stress tests". Firstly, there was the financial crisis of 2008, than a migration and asylum crisis followed by a security crisis and finally BREXIT in June 2016 when the book was finished. How to explain the paradox of the absence of European citizenship from these crises when it should have been invoked as a means to overcome them?

The search for European citizenship is a search for an organising framework. This was lacking and could not be found in the dispersed official initiatives invoking European citizen. It was above all from being exposed to the scholarship around European citizenship and learning from several research projects covering different disciplines, that it became possible to write this book. The key to finding European citizenship was the lesson from the scholars that citizenship at any level is about rights, access and belonging. I am confident of being on firm ground in that this lesson fits with lessons learnt through practical experience. The guidelines attached on European Citizens' Rights, Involvement and Trust is an attempt to put forward an organising framework.

On 10 July 2015, Foundation Charles Leopold Meyer (FPH) and their publishing house Editions Charles Leopold Meyer (ECLM) organised a brainstorming meeting to discuss the book and the follow up to the guidelines. The argument and case for a holistic approach to European citizenship was supported. The organisations present included those such as European Alternatives and the European Civic Forum which had played their part in the 2013 European Year of Citizens Alliance (EYCA) which had advocated a similar approach to this book. How though could the guidelines be implemented? A first step should be to bring activists, academics and policy makers together at a summer university. Consideration should also be given to launching a European citizens' initiative whereby one million citizens from a significant number of the 28 EU Member States can sign a demand to be put on the agenda of the European Union - a demand to make much more of European citizenship.

Table of Content

Acknowledgments

The book could not have been written without the help of Amanda Cleary, my wife, who is a lawyer specialised in the European Treaties. My daughter Alicia Cleary-Venables contributed to some of the earlier drafts and did the final proof reading. I am also very grateful to Pamela Piech and Federica Chiarella who provided assistance with editing, up-dating and referencing and to Peter Téglas, who discovered interesting material and provided academic guidance. When the first draft was completed in autumn 2015 it was reviewed by Antoine Fobe a former colleague who has more experience with advising citizens how to enforce their European rights than anyone else I know and who put right misinterpretations of European law and added new points. He also provided valuable insights on the implication of BREXIT. Equally extensive was the review by Inga Wachsmann from FPH who suggested a fuller treatment of the role of civil society. I am deeply indebted to these two experts for their insights and the improvements they made.

I would like to thank the following people who over the years have educated me, made comments on the attached guidelines on European citizenship, or contributed directly to this book with ideas, sources, etc.: Chiara Adamo, Onno Brower, Alain Brun, Claire Damilano, Virgilio Dastoli, Andrew Duff, Pietro Emili, Justin Greenwood, Gerald Häfner, Jean Lambert, Angela Liberatore, Paul Magnette, Alfonso Mattera, Niccolo Milanese, Mario Monti, Giovanni Moro, Rodolphe Munoz, Nick Perks, Stephen Pittam, Ettore Recchi, Jo Shaw, Richard Upson and Simone Veil.

INTRODUCTION
The structure of the book and case for a holistic approach to European citizenship

The message of this book is that European citizenship is too scattered an affair, meaning so many different things to different people that it can end up as an abstraction. Yet, to meet the challenges facing Europe, whether internal or external, our rights and duties towards others are being put to the test, or put another way the scope and limits of our sense of being not just a national but also a European citizen. Over the last eight years of economic and financial crisis, what should be the extent of taxpayer solidarity from the stronger economic regions towards the weaker ones? To what extent are threats from Russia spreading from the Ukraine to the Baltic States an issue for neighbouring countries or Europe as a whole? To what extent are the deaths of thousands of asylum seekers and migrants trying to reach our shores on all our consciences or primarily a responsibility for the countries bordering on the Mediterranean and Adriatic seas? To reach agreement among 28 governments, the EU Institutions appear incapable of doing more than contain crises, rather than solve them and offer perspectives for the future. The political will to appeal to more European solidarity is being sapped by the rise of the extreme right and excessive nationalism, which can all too easily spill over to racism and xenophobia. What else can hold Europe together but a common sense of shared citizenship beyond borders? Is it out of deference to national sovereignty that European citizenship does not dare to speak its name?

At first sight, European citizenship appears an unlikely basis on which to build the future of the European Union, if limited to its official definition in Articles 18-25 of the Treaty on the functioning of the European Union (TFEU).These are essentially the rights to equal treatment and to move freely within the European Union to which are attached limited political rights in one's country of residence. The right to petition the European Parliament, appeal to the European ombudsman, and more recently to propose a legislative initiative backed by 1 million signatures seek to give the citizen more of a voice in EU decision-making. Rights to consular protection outside the Union are also being developed.This summary overlooks the fact that other parts of the Treaties, legislation and policies create a mosaic of a citizenship which was intended originally to be linked to all the policies of the Union. In this introduction, the case for a more holistic approach to European citizenship is developed. The disadvantage of an approach which is scattered in the EU Institutions is that European citizenship is exported in pieces and seen from different vantage points by civil society and academic disciplines, even though one lesson from scholarship related to citizenship is that its different components stand or fall together. The advantage of bringing the different pieces together is that European citizenship begins to become more substantial than in its official definition. It also becomes apparent where there are gaps and where reforms are necessary, which should be similarly connected. The holistic approach is reflected in the guidelines attached to this book. In the first part of this introduction, the structure of the book is summarised and in the second the case for a holistic approach to European citizenship is argued.

(i) The structure of the book

In Part One "Searching for Cinderella," it is shown that through an expanding set of Treaty provisions, standards and practices, European citizenship is at a stage where a sound basis exists for such a holistic approach to be developed. European citizenship is like Cinderella before she went to the ball and was discovered by the prince. It is a status of great potential, yet to be popular. In the first three chapters, this claim is substantiated from three perspectives-historical, legal and everyday practice:

Chapter 1: How did European citizenship emerge in the context of the European Union?

This first transnational citizenship of the modern era was not just invented by the Maastricht Treaty in 1993, barely a generation ago, but can be traced back to the early period of European integration, even much earlier. Just as Saint Paul could appeal as a Roman citizen to be tried in Rome, so an EU citizen now can appeal to a national court if his or her European rights are infringed and the case referred to the Court of Justice of the European Union. At the outset free movement of people was limited to free movement of workers, first in the coal and steel industries and then in all sectors, before being extended to the self-employed, students and pensioners. And, this early history is not only about progressing from a fragmented approach towards a citizenship of rights, but also about attempts to forge a peoples' Europe including such aims as to create a European passport and eliminate internal border controls.

Chapter 2: How did European citizenship progress, particularly as a result of the Court of Justice of the European Union?

When the Maastricht Treaty was ratified in 1993 opinions diverged on the meaning of Union citizenship – a public relations exercise or the beginning of a citizenship in its own right. The case-law developed by the European Court from Martinez Sala (Case C-85/96) to Ruiz Zambrano (Case C-34/09) described here in detail has made Union citizenship "a fundamental status of nationals of Member States", and settled the early argument (if uneasily) somewhere between the two extremes. A European right to free movement has become a genuine citizenship right detached from its economic origins. European citizenship can be invoked in a court against barriers to freedom of movement in such sensitive areas as access to social benefits, educational loans, immigration policies or even the loss or acquisition of citizenship itself.[1]

Chapter 3: European rights to free movement: both extensively practiced and controversial.

Europe is on the move and to a greater extent than suggested by the official figures of 13.5 million European citizens living and working in other Member States alongside 21 million third country nationals. This is because atypical and short-term unrecorded movements are not taken into account: nor is the extent of physical or virtual interaction with people of other countries, reaching some 30% of the 509 million people in the EU.

---

1 Some readers may find chapter 3 on the case law on the Court of Justice of the European Union too detailed. We believe, however, that this is necessary to develop a clear sense of the scope and limits of European rights and how they can be better defended by referring to the case law. In reality it is the Court which has taken the lead in giving substance to European citizenship even though it has become recently much more cautious.

Sociological Europe, particularly among those of the younger generation who travel and have language skills is ahead of political Europe. Nevertheless, free movement is bound up with the internal and external challenges facing the EU itself, and is under threat from scare-mongering and the public perception of the failure of migration policies. The "status quo" can no longer be taken for granted. For example future negotiations between the UK and the EU following BREXIT could well result in a resounding declaration about a victory for upholding the principle of free movement, whilst in practice putting in place more restrictions on access to welfare benefits which remain hidden from view. To some extent this is already happening.

Chapter 4: What wide-open challenges for the future of European citizenship?

Given these solid foundations, why has more not been done to develop European citizenship? In the final chapter of part one, the challenges facing this citizenship are explored in relation to its popularity or otherwise, the reluctance of governments and the tensions with national citizenship. We go on to ask how well does European citizenship fit with the decision-making processes of the European Union? Could a broader European rather than just an EU citizenship emerge one day based on shared values?

In Part Two "finding Cinderella", these challenges are taken up in the following chapters (5-7), based on the guidelines for European citizens' Rights, Involvement and Trust.

Chapter 5: Mind the gaps - how can European citizens' rights be better enforced and enlarged ?

In theory, if citizenship is the right to have rights, European citizenship has solid foundations. There is though a gap between the fine principles of European rights and how they are applied. In the first section, recommendations are made to close this gap and improve enforcement: a one stop-shop in each country, more emphasis on prevention, collective redress for citizens and quicker action to lift barriers. A European free movement solidarity fund is also proposed. European citizens' rights should be placed in the broader context of the EU Charter of Fundamental Rights, but here too there is a gap between the fine aims and application in practice, which needs clarification. Such steps should be taken before embarking on any radical expansion of rights.

It is though difficult to understand why some political rights attached to free movement (to vote and stand in municipal and European elections) are granted, whereas others (particularly to vote in national elections) are denied. This is the theme of the second section. Another issue is the lack of equal treatment between European citizens and long-term resident third country nationals. In the third section, reasons for putting equal treatment for all migrants in Europe back on the political agenda are argued.

Chapter 6: How can access and involvement of citizens to the EU
          Institutions be made more effective?

In theory, just as the European Union has a comprehensive framework of rights, so it also offers, more than any other international organisation, a range of opportunities for citizens to come forward with their claims. In some cases, there is a conscious effort to reach citizens and the channels of communication are mobilised by civil society organisations. Much of the routine decision-making – for example the current EU "better regu-lation agenda"- is however an obstacle to citizen involvement because of the technical nature of policy-making and standards-setting as well as the procedural complexities of the legislative process. The result is that pro-cesses designed with citizens in mind have in reality become captured by experts, and well-entrenched lobbyists. The main theme in this chapter is how to restore a bigger space to the citizen. In the first section, it is pro-posed that the right of access to documents should become a right to free-dom of information, which implies that the EU would offer more assis-tance to citizens to identify the documents they need. In the second sec-tion, it is recognised that the growth in professional lobbying around the EU has become a deterrent to citizen involvement but at least the lobbying process should become more transparent, and the register of interest groups mandatory and accurate. In the third section, ways are recommend-ed to make consultation processes better known – more accessible and multi-lingual. Whilst these reforms are necessary, they are unlikely to be enough, so that further ways to involve citizens have to be considered.

Chapter 7: How to develop European citizenship by strengthening
participatory and representative democracy?

In introducing principles of participatory and representative democracy in
the Lisbon Treaty, the EU recognises that previous steps taken towards
European governance based on openness had failed to engage citizens.[2] In
the first section of this chapter, we examine whether the participatory
democracy toolbox (e.g. citizens' assemblies, consultations, juries etc.)
works at European level. This has been shown to be a promising way to
include citizens in processes otherwise dominated by expert consultations
and lobbying, but it should be embedded in EU decision-making processes. The second section examines what has been the experience so far with
the introduction of the European Citizens' Initiative (ECI) whereby over 1
million signatures from a minimum of 7 Member States can be collected
within 12 months in support of a proposed EU law. This first ever transnational instrument of deliberative democracy has made a faltering start with
a high failure rate either because the initiative was rejected at the outset by
the Commission as being outside its legal competence or because the organisers had insufficient resources to collect the necessary signatures.[3]
The third section examines what lessons can be learned from the form of
participation to which people attach the most importance: voting in a poll
with a real choice of policies and candidates to represent them. What
lessons can be learned about voter turnout, and ways to make the elections
more European, for example by introducing transnational party lists? The
European elections of May 2014 did introduce more choice of the leading
European candidates for Commission President. This first success should
be built upon and encourage further reforms for the next elections in 2019.

---

2 Throughout this book reference is made to the Lisbon Treaty. However, the Lisbon
Treaty consists of two previous Treaties which it amended: Treaty on European
Union (TEU) and the Treaty on the Functioning of the European Union (TFEU).
For the original documents go to: http://eur-lex.europa.eu/legal-content/EN/TXT/?
uri=CELEX:12007L/TXT,   http://eur-lex.europa.eu/legal-content/EN/TXT/?
uri=celex:12012E/TXT

3 Regulation (EU) no 211/2011 of 16 February 2011 on the citizens' initiative (Official Journal L65 of 11.3.2011). For an overview, see the Commission's register of
initiatives and guide. 3 ECIs so far reached the 1 million threshold, 15 did not, 20
were refused at the outset and 8 were withdrawn. Currently there are only 3 new
ECIs running.

Chapter 8: Once found, can Cinderella acquire more universal appeal?

Here, we go back to the broader issues of trust and participation raised by the chapter on challenges of European citizenship and attempt to answer the question of how to make this a citizenship for all and one of civic equality. "Institutional reform of the EU will fail to register with Member States nationals if they have not first become more active citizens and self-conscious inhabitants of a European public space".[4] One answer lies in a proposal for a right to be informed because the "right to have rights" depends on knowing that they exist in the first place. Another could be to build courses on European citizenship in civic education, which has recently spread across geographical Europe. Awareness of being a European citizen has to start young and be developed through the teaching of history and languages; this has been addressed in a European perspective only to a limited extent so far, and with marked differences across the Member States. Citizenship needs symbols. For European citizens the symbol could be a card including existing rights and which gives everyone an additional right to once-in-a-lifetime participation in an EU exchange or study programme. Such reforms could make European citizenship both more popular and more equal, but to give it real substance active support across civil society is essential.

In the conclusions, the reforms proposed are listed in a 12 point action plan – Would individual proposals really make a difference? Not enough – collectively they could, in a new contract between the EU and European citizens. If such reforms had been put in place, the EU would have managed these crises better and more democratically and the UK might not have voted on 23 June 2016 to leave the EU.

(ii) The case for a holistic approach to European citizenship

What is European citizenship? Inevitably people see this first transnational citizenship of the modern era through the lens of their national citizenships with all their diversity in terms of history, geography, the organisation of

---

4 Perez-Diaz, V. cited in Warleigh, A. "Making Citizens from the Market? NGOs and the Representation of Interests?" in Bellamy, R., Castiglione, D., Shaw, J. (eds) *Making European Citizens: Civic Inclusion in a Transnational Context.* Basingstoke: Palgrave Macmillan, pp. 118-133, 2006.

the State, culture and language. And not just between countries, but within our own country, our views on citizenship differ, so that if one day we come to share a common citizenship it could only be a melting pot of different liberal rights, republican or communitarian approaches.[5] In the meantime, our different backgrounds and approaches are resulting in increasing fragmentation of public opinion about difficult issues for citizenship such as migration, religious tolerance and freedom of expression. Is citizenship a way of linking different communities and identities – a multicultural approach – or is it to do with forging a common identity? European citizenship poses such questions and many others:

- To what extent is European citizenship an extension of our nationality and transnational through the opening up of our respective territories and citizenships to each other, or a genuinely post-national citizenship with its own existence?
- Should the rights attached to European citizenship be limited to nationals of EU Member States or extended to all those legally resident in the EU? What is the relationship between European rights and universal rights in the UN Charter, the Council of Europe Convention on Human Rights or the European Union's Charter of Fundamental Rights?
- How to make European citizenship work properly and close the gap between the fine principles of these conventions and the way people, especially those who are vulnerable, are treated in practice? What reforms are necessary to enforce rights?
- How well does the concept of citizenship fit with the Institutions and different decision-making processes of the EU? Will citizens really have a voice through existing channels dominated by expertise and lobbies? How to ensure that expectations created by the promise of involvement are not disappointed as the recent failure of European citizens' initiatives suggests?
- How to educate from an early age, communicate and involve for a European citizenship based on mutual trust and which belongs to all? Like the European Union itself, is not European citizenship too much

---

5 Liberals advocate the *citizenship-as-rights* model, communitarians promote the *citizenship-as-belonging* model, whereas republicans embrace the *citizenship-as-participation* model. See: Bellamy, R., Castiglione D., and Shaw, J. (eds.) "Introduction: From National to Transnational Citizenship' in *Making European Citizens: Civic Inclusion in a Transnational Context.* Basingstoke: Palgrave Macmillan, pp. 1-31, 2006.

of an elite driven project? Its advantages are enjoyed by a relatively privileged, mobile, well-educated and linguistically competent few, excluding those less fortunate.

– Could a broader European citizenship be conceived, based not so much on a fixed territory but shared values and capable of resisting the downward spiral of extreme nationalism and xenophobia?

– Could there be a European citizenship linked to the EU which includes residents and not only nationals of Member States but also those of neighbouring countries?

The fascination but also the frustration of dealing with such questions is that one keeps going back inevitably to "what is European citizenship?" in the first place, only to find a void. No single person or group can provide an answer, which could only come from the involvement of citizens themselves across national and citizenship borders over at least a generation. The problem though is to find a common starting point, which is the aim of this book with its Guidelines for European Rights, Involvement and Trust. The book itself, particularly in Part II sets out to explore to what extent such guidelines are already in existence, could be better enforced and what more should be done. The basic thesis is that we cannot begin to answer the question "what is European citizenship?" because its components are far too scattered. A more holistic approach is necessary.

At first sight, a narrow interpretation of the Treaties would result in associating Union citizenship with rights triggered by crossing a border. That would, however, mean ignoring the original intentions and rights scattered in other parts of the Treaties. Free movement of people is only the starting point. According to Article 20 of the Treaty on the Functioning of the European Union (TFEU) under the heading "Non-discrimination and Citizenship of the Union," "Citizenship of the Union is hereby established. Every person holding the nationality of a Member State shall be a citizen of the Union. Citizenship of the Union shall be additional to and not replace national citizenship". It should be noted that citizenship is not limited here to any particular set of policies or rights, such as those to free movement, so that in principle nothing would exclude a more holistic approach. Under this chapter, 508 million people acquire a number of rights as European citizens:

– to be treated equally and not to be discriminated against on the grounds of nationality,

- to receive protection against all other forms of discrimination on the basis of sex, racial or ethnic origin, religion or belief, disability, age or sexual orientation,
- to move and reside freely within the territory of the Member State, subject to certain conditions,
- to vote and stand as candidates in elections to the European Parliament and in municipal elections in their Member State of residence,
- to receive protection from diplomatic and consular authorities in any country outside the Union in which their Member State is not represented,
- to petition the European Parliament, to apply to the European ombudsman and address an EU Institution in their own language and receive a reply in the same language,
- to organise or support an initiative whereby over 1 million European citizens can demand new European legislation.

In the preface to the report on European citizenship during the European Year of Citizens in 2013 Viviane Reding, Vice President of the European Commission wrote: "European citizenship is the cornerstone of EU integration. It should be to political union what the Euro is to economic and monetary union." [6] Indeed, citizenship was added to the Maastricht Treaty at the same time as economic and monetary union. How though can the quotation above be understood when the same report she prefaced defines European citizenship only on the basis of the limited section on citizenship and non-discrimination in the Treaties? The report itself makes no link to economic and monetary union, although it followed five years of headline news about whether the euro would survive the crisis. This is just one example of the way European citizenship is seen as an aspiration and political rhetoric, which is not translated into reality.

When in 1992 on the initiative of the Spanish government "Union citizenship" was first added as a revision to the Maastricht Treaty, the intention was to bring together all the different rights which are scattered in different parts of the EU Treaties. It was not the intention of the Spanish government that a limited set of essentially free movement rights agreed at Maastricht should constitute Union citizenship; rather this should be a first

---

6 European Commission. *EU Citizenship Report 2013*. Frequent reference is made to the reports produced every three years by the Commission on Union citizenship. For *EU Citizenship Report 2010* go to: http://ec.europa.eu/justice/citizen/files/com_2010_603_en.pdf.

step of an "evolving dimension" since a "genuine Union will logically require full-scale European citizenship." [7] European citizenship was seen as a dynamic process, "which should inform all the policies of the Union." The aim was to bring together all the specific rights across the Treaties for example by establishing "a Charter on rights of the citizens which would constitute a "catalogue" of rights to be implemented through legal texts at a later stage".[8] Policy makers should therefore go back to the spirit of the original idea for European citizenship as an evolving concept which was watered down in the Treaty negotiations.[9] That does imply though a further revision of the Treaties. Article 25 (TFEU) requires the assent of the European Parliament and unanimity in the Council of Ministers for the addition of new European rights. A necessary reform would be to enable use of the normal legislative process with the European Parliament able to amend proposals and decisions taken by majority in the Council.[10] One of the lessons of history is that real progress towards citizenship is made when the normal decision-making process is used.

The list of rights in Articles 18-25 TFEU remains incomplete. The main focus is on rights linked to free movement within the EU, but not exclusively. So why ignore other EU rights which can be invoked without movement to another Member State? For example, gender equality and equal pay for equal work (Art. 157) could well figure alongside the strong commitment to forbid discrimination on the grounds of nationality (Art. 18). Similarly, whilst the official definition of European citizenship includes the right to petition the European Parliament and complain to the European ombudsman – a post created by the Maastricht Treaty – it is

---

7 SN2614/90; and SN4811/90 (non-paper). The idea of the guidelines in this book is also in line with the original proposals for Union citizenship in contributions by the Spanish delegation to the inter-governmental conference on European citizenship. Documents: 2614/90, SN 3940/90, SN 4811/90, CONF-UP 1731/91, CONF-UP 1807/91, CONF-UP 1800/91.Thanks to the Secretariat of the Council of Ministers this package of documents was supplied following a request made under the access to documents regulation.

8 Ibid. - see 9.

9 The article requiring the Commission to report every three years on the development of Union citizenship and make appropriate proposals (now Article 25) was the first in the order of the original proposal, but became the last in the agreed Treaty text. The Article is referred to frequently in this book. See Article 25: http://eur-lex.europa.eu/legal-content/EN/ TXT/?uri=celex:12012E/TXT.

10 See Article 294 of the TFEU on co-decision procedure: http://eur-lex.europa.eu/ legal- ontent/EN/TXT/?uri=celex:12012E/TXT.

elsewhere in the Treaty that the closely related right of access to documents can be found (Article 15). The most recent reform by the Treaty of Lisbon also makes the Charter of Fundamental Rights legally binding placing European citizenship in a broader framework of universal, traditional and more modern economic and social rights and rights to environmental, social, consumer and public health protection. The process of approximation of national laws in order to create the internal market and an area of freedom, justice and security also provide contexts in which to develop European citizenship. This book argues for an attempt to bring together all the scattered parts of the Treaties, legislation and standards related to European citizenship. There is a further argument for such a step: European citizenship should follow Treaty reforms which have abolished a former structure of policies round three pillars (the traditional EU flanked by home affairs and justice on the one hand, foreign policy on the other) and fused them together.

This argument may well be greeted with the sceptical response: does this matter? What would be the added value of attempting to bring together the different elements of European citizenship? At a time of growing public opposition to the European project, the focus of the European Institutions is on immediate practical impact and results, rather than on long-term concepts. One can argue that history is in any case on the side of European, even global citizenship developing naturally by practice. Our sense of being a citizen has developed from our village to the city to the nation and beyond. The extent of our interconnectedness is becoming increasingly apparent as more is revealed about our origins and patterns of migration. Citizenship has to catch up with the accelerating pace of collective decision-making by governments, so apparent in the fragility of the global financial system, climate change or security threats. [11] A form of rooted cosmopolitanism is now possible thanks to social media, cheaper travel and the emergence of a better educated class across the world able to share and act on the same concerns across borders. In a publication by European Alternatives "The transeuropa caravans - connecting local alternative voices" what it means be a citizen is defined as follows:

> *"A citoyen per definition is someone, in the spirit of the age of enlightenment, who cares for his or her community, respecting the common good. It is someone who takes charge of finding solutions (local to global) independently and*

---

11 Held, D. *Models of Democracy*. 3rd ed. Cambridge: Polity Press, 2006.

puts them into practice. Naturally, he or she inspires others to do the same and plants the seeds for larger societal change".[12]

Acts of citizenship will create a common citizenship from the bottom-up. Often however, governments and the traditional political parties appear remote and disconnected from this spread of local to international acts of citizenship and democracy. In turn, acts of citizenship are often disconnected from each other, lack impact and continuity and a sense of shared citizenship among not just the active and the activists, but also the passive. It is argued in the last chapter that an activist civil society should become the carrier of European citizenship, but it is not one which can work on its own without institutional reforms in response to its demands. A shared consensus of what European citizenship is could help forge alliances among civil society organisations, academics and policy makers.

A more fundamental objection to the argument that European citizenship should simply take its course is the recent rise of nationalism and euroscepticism. This is not the same as racism and xenophobia but excessive nationalism can all too easily spill over towards their acceptance in common, open or coded discourse led by populist movements and politicians. The interconnectedness revealed by the economic and financial crisis over the last eight years has had for some the opposite effect to the search for a citizenship beyond the nation, an equally understandable retreat to the citizenship one knows best with its guarantees of protection by the state, however uncertain, in the areas of education, health, social benefits and pensions for example. For many, citizenship does not only fail to fit with the European Institutions, but its most cherished entitlements are under threat from "austerity" and Europe. The rise of right wing nationalism is the main driver of the increase in the representation of euro-sceptical parties, which are now a substantial minority in the European Parliament following the 2014 elections. European citizenship is potentially a powerful counterbalance to the re-emergence of nationalism. For that to happen there is no alternative to working towards a clearer understanding of what it is, so it becomes a shared responsibility.

In different ways, the tensions between the two citizenships are at the heart of the challenges facing Europe and the European Union. When Union citizenship was added to the EU Treaties at Maastricht, at the same time as economic and monetary union, one of the aims was that it should

---

12   For more information go to: https://euroalter.com/projects/citizens-pact.

counteract the danger of an increasingly technocratic and purely economic construction. With the onslaught of the financial and Euro crisis in 2008, European citizenship has been largely irrelevant, except for its offer to job seekers in countries hardest hit to find work in the more prosperous economies. One effect, however, of the crisis and the headline news of repeated heads of government meetings, has been to reveal the extent of interconnectedness and create a European public sphere. This though is a sphere of centrifugal forces, depending on whether it concerns being a citizen of a country contributing to bail-outs, on the receiving end of loans with often unacceptable conditions attached, or on the margins or outside the Eurozone, but nevertheless aware of how relevant the handling of the crisis is to one's own future. It is not surprising therefore that a European Union agreement was reached in July 2015 to keep Greece in the euro zone and which appears to satisfy no-one. A European issue became a national one with Greece's creditors agreeing on a lowest common denominator and tough line resulting in a clash between the dictates of the single currency and the democratic decisions taken by the Greek people in elections and a referendum.

The limits of a European citizenship, which is too weak and scattered to create a sense of Europe-wide solidarity and shared values, was apparent in 2015 when the EU faced not one but several crises with very different geographical impacts, despite the fact that all had continental-scale implications. The tragedy of thousands of deaths of migrants trying to reach Europe's shores has resonated across the continent but has had more impact on the Southern and Eastern States than the Northern States, again the effect being Europe-wide but not necessarily unifying. In turn, public opinion appeared more divided than sharing the same European values, even though the image of one dead child on a beach resonated across the continent. As a result, the reactions of governments were chaotically divergent, some building fences and closing borders, others working with their neighbours. Why for example was the UK so much less generous than Germany in receiving asylum seekers?

The Commission is doing what it can to promote a Europe-wide approach-for example by burden-sharing and a quota system for the resettlement of asylum seekers, only to be overtaken by the rapid growth in demands and disagreements about managing external Schengen borders. This in turn has led the Commission to put forward proposals for a European border and coastguard, which have been supported by some governments and rejected by others.[13]

The lack of a united response to the pressures of asylum and migration together with the terrorist attacks in Paris on 13 November 2015 placed new strains on the Schengen system of open borders within the EU. It can be argued that open borders are here to stay since only eight states have re-instated intra-EU Schengen border controls on a temporary basis.[14] The government of the Netherlands proposed a mini-Schengen, a suggestion immediately rejected by the new Member States in Central and Eastern Europe. The future of one of the EU's most popular but also controversial achievements is under threat with not just controls but also walls and fences at some borders and the risk that temporary controls might become permanent.

For the first time since the end of the Cold War, Europe appears vulnerable to external threats. To what extent however, do people in the North and South of Europe share the same concerns as those in the new EU Member States of Central and Eastern Europe about the threat from Russia in the Ukraine and the Baltic States where they have minority populations? In one way or another, the challenges facing Europe pose questions of the extent and limits of solidarity. How can these challenges be tackled effectively if governments can only represent their national parliaments and electorates, rather than the European dimension of citizenship at the same time? The impacts of the challenges facing the European Union seen purely from the standpoint of national citizenship are so uneven as to render the common interest less visible, whereas meeting them depends on such a perception and public support.

---

13 "COM(2015)671 final of 15.12.2015 on the European Border and Coast Guard.", 2015.

14 Guild, E., Brouwer, E., Groenendijk, K, Carrera, S. "What is happening to the Schengen Borders? CEPS Paper in Liberty and Security in Europe", No. 86, 2015. Available from: https://www.ceps.eu/publications/what-happening-schengen-borders. In a communication "Back to Schengen –A roadmap" (Com (2016)120 final of 4 March 2016), the European Commission estimates that full reinstatement of internal border controls would cost the EU between 5 and 18 billion euros annually. The Commission recommends that temporary border controls introduced because of migratory pressures by Austria, Belgium, Denmark, Germany, Hungary, Norway, Slovenia and Sweden should be phased out and Schengen returned to normal functioning with more secure external borders by the end of 2016.

In this context, it is certain that the scattered nature of the approaches and policies to deliver on European citizenship does matter and has a weakening side-lining effect.

The scattered approach to European citizenship by the EU Institutions, civil society and the research community.

European Institutions.

In the first place, one would expect the lead to come from the European Institutions, especially since the case-law of the Court of Justice of the European Union has created a citizenship in its own right and a "fundamental status". In reality, competences for European citizenship are scattered in the European Institutions. Inevitably this means that a rights-based agenda predominates and has been developed further than other aspects of citizenship. Even here, the approach in the Commission is fragmented with free movement and residence rights coming under the Commission's departments for home affairs and justice, work and social security under employment and social affairs, recognition of professional qualifications under the internal market whereas the exchange programmes and institutional provisions to do with access to the EU by citizens are dealt with elsewhere. A step towards a more holistic approach was taken in the former European Commission from 2009-2014 when Viviane Reding occupied the post of Vice-President responsible for justice, fundamental rights and citizenship. In the new Commission (2014-2019), however, responsibilities appear even more scattered. Since it is from the Commission that all legislative and policy initiatives come, it is only from here that the official approach to Union citizenship can be more or less holistic or piecemeal. In theory, since Vice Presidents have a coordinating role over teams of Commissioners, Frans Timmermans could take on a role as the Vice President for European citizenship and successor to Viviane Reding.

In the European Parliament, which is the institution directly elected and therefore most accountable to citizens, responsibilities are equally divided due to the predominant role of specialised committees for civil liberties, employment and social affairs, the internal market or culture and education. This approach is also reflected in different committees of experts in the Council of Ministers. It is difficult to avoid the conclusion that the EU structures and administrative culture are still based on an earlier period where people were divided by category of the population, age, gender or occupation. The EU has difficulty in relating to citizens per se, even though there are some promising moves in that direction discussed at the end of this introduction.

Civil society

In theory, nothing would prevent civil society and researchers from accepting the need for the Commission as both initiator of legislation and guardian of the Treaty to adopt a targeted and specialised approach, whilst developing a more holistic one for their own purposes. In practice, however, the Commission both sets the agenda for the legislative debate and in the non-legislative area through its funding of exchange programmes, civil society and research projects, influences how stakeholders respond. Can civil society organisations (CSOs) bring in a more holistic citizenship dimension?[15] The dilemma is that CSOs are often at their most effective when representing a particular category of the population or a single issue, rather than more general cross-cutting concerns such as citizenship. When Union citizenship was added to the Maastricht Treaty it was very much a top-down initiative. The attention of civil society was directed elsewhere towards the addition of specific new areas of activity to the EU: public health, consumer protection, culture, education and youth and new elements of social and environmental policy. In retrospect, this strategic focus on more sectoral policies may have been misguided. Union citizenship has since developed more significantly and acquired greater legal sub-

---

15 Civil society is part of the Third Sector. The Third Sector – the peoples' sector- is distinct from the other two: government and commerce. Its roots lie in citizens associating freely together, both to advocate for a common cause with the powers that be and to meet unmet needs, particularly to protect the most vulnerable in society. Covering all areas of human endeavour, the third sector is about change and takes on a wide variety of organisational forms from voluntary associations to civil society and the social economy. It ranges from the local to the global, from self-help to philanthropic ventures. Beneath the surface of such apparent diversity, third sector organisations strive to achieve participation of their members and commitment to a broader public interest. They also share common values of solidarity, respect for human rights and the rule of law, including the right and duty to defend freedom of association itself, as a guarantee that such values will be upheld.

stance than the softer competences added at Maastricht. There remains though the difficulty that for CSOs to be effective advocates, they need interlocutors and there is no single one for European citizenship.

There are therefore barriers to civil society taking on a role as advance guard for the cause of European citizenship:

   – *The difficulty of reaching consensus and creating a coalition.*

Given the tendency for CSOs to opt for a single issue or clear focus, effective advocacy for European citizenship requires coalition building. But this is not easy, since many associations especially those working in the area of migrants' rights have doubts about a citizenship which distinguishes between EU nationals who have this status and "third country nationals" who do not. Civil society organisations have much to offer through their particular expertise and strongly held views, but it is not easy to bring them together. Even more general purpose organisations have to specialise in rights, participation or civic education for example. There are even two quite separate communities of interest round citizen participatory practices (chapter 7 section 1) and European citizens initiatives (section 2) even though the two are simply means to the same end of giving citizens an increasing role in European affairs. Coalitions or umbrella organisations exist generally to mediate among such differences, but often struggle for sufficient time and resources to achieve more than agreement on paper.

   – *The lack of an interlocutor in the EU Institutions.*

In reality it is misleading to see the third sector which includes civil society as completely independent from the other two - government and private enterprise. To be effective CSOs need allies in the administration which can deliver. In the environmental sector for example this condition is met with a European level administration, a specialised parliamentary committee and regular meetings of environmental ministers - a powerful legislative decision-making process. Progress is achieved by more or less explicit alliances between non-governmental organisations and officials or elected representatives (often to try to counterbalance private sector lobbying). Environmental associations come together as the "Green 10". In areas which impact on European citizenship by contrast the interlocutors are numerous small units lacking power and struggling with parts of a jigsaw within larger administrations which have other responsibilities such as justice, security, migration, the internal market or education. Thus subsumed, European citizenship as such is everyone's and no-one's responsibility and has to struggle for political support. Given the weak and scattered institutional context it is surprising how often the term "European citizen" is used in official EU discourse.

— *Lack of resources for European citizenship.*

It follows that funding for aspects of European citizenship is small scale and scattered. In chapter 7 for example we point out that the failure of citizens' initiatives is as much due to lack of economic viability as to the over complex requirements for signature collection. The "Europe for Citizens Programme" is the poor relation among all EU programmes, providing just 25 million euros per year for small scale projects involving meetings with citizens around two broad strands of activity - "European remembrance" and "Democratic engagement and civil participation".[16] A number of operating grants are given to pro-European associations such as the European movement and think-tanks. To support European citizenship, there should be a change to the Europe for citizens programme with less emphasis on grants and more on the creation of a European public sphere to connect individual initiatives.

Despite these barriers we go back in the last chapter to consider in more detail the role civil society could play by bringing together a broad coalition round the concept of European citizenship.

The research community.

In the absence of a clear narrative for European citizenship either from the European Institutions or civil society, the research community has both highlighted the gaps whilst being placed in a difficult position to overcome the fragmented approach to European citizenship. Departments commissioning research tend to concentrate on a specific aspect of European citizenship within their competence. This may well match a particular academic discipline or set of interests whether in the area of European law, political science, sociology – but also history, philosophy, geography and other disciplines. Under the European framework programme for research,

---

16 For more information on the Europe for Citizens Programme go to: http://ec.europa.eu/citizenship/europe-for-citizens-programme/index_en.htm.

Horizon 2020, large-scale multi-disciplinary approaches are developed.[17] Despite such attempts, one can distinguish different circles of interest and research communities round the rights-based approach to citizenship, European citizenship and the public sphere, or the broader cultural issues of identity and a sense of belonging. These correspond in turn to academic disciplines and specialised publications providing outlets for research. One can well speculate that the elusiveness of European citizenship and its scattered nature has probably stimulated a more impressive research output about what it is and might become, than if there was more consensus. On the other hand, the multi-disciplinary approach is the exception rather than the rule and this overlooks one of the main lessons coming from scholarship on citizenship and democracy: the different aspects of European like any other citizenship are linked.

The lack therefore of a community of interest round European citizenship.

On specific policy or legislative initiatives, circles of interest are developed and there is cross-fertilisation among the various actors in the EU Institutions, civil society and academia. An example is the community of interest which has grown round European citizens' inititiatives (ECIs). There is however, no community of interest when it comes to the basic questions of European citizenship itself. This was apparent for example in 2013 when the European Union organised its special year of citizens to celebrate the 20th anniversary of the inclusion of Union citizenship in the Maastricht Treaty. For the EU Institutions, the main purpose was to raise awareness of European rights. For a broad alliance of civil society organisations, the year "should not be confined to an individual rights approach, but should have a strong value-based dimension", with citizenship a theme cutting across all EU policy areas. A third strand was more political: a series of Commission sponsored town-hall meetings with citizens across the 28 EU Member States to discuss the future of Europe in the run-up to the 2014 European elections. With a more holistic approach it would have been possible to bring all three pathways together as complementary to illustrate different facets of European citizenship. Instead, they appeared

---

17 BEUCITIZEN is the current and onlylarge-scale research project led by the University of Utrecht. See: http://beucitizen.eu/.

diffuse, unrelated and the year made little impact. At the beginning of 2013 the results of a European survey showing the progress made in education for citizenship and human rights across Europe was published.[18] It would however have been a challenge for any teacher to extract from the year material to explain what European citizenship is.

The current scattered approach to European citizenship therefore has disadvantages, leading to underestimation of what it is, even invisibility. At the same time, policy fragmentation undermines the possibility of creating a multi-disciplinary and cross-sectoral community of interest. It does not however necessarily follow that a more holistic approach would make an immediate impact. Citizenship can be fostered and encouraged, but there is no single measure or quick fix like turning on the tap. There are three reasons however why such an approach should be tried:

— *What exists under the different components of citizenship becomes more visible and powerful.* In the guidelines for European citizens' Rights, Involvement and Trust, the aim is to reach beyond the narrow focus of Union citizenship in Articles 18-25 of TEFU and bring in elements scattered in other parts of the Treaty, policies and programmes. The European Union has certainly gone further towards a rights-based citizenship. The other two components should be given more priority especially since they risk being overshadowed by high profile court cases and the political debates around rights to freedom of movement and migration policies. By bringing all three together in the guidelines, it does become apparent that more progress has been made – or at least groundwork laid – to building a European citizenship and creating European citizens than might otherwise be thought. The reader will also find examples of where European reforms have had a multiplier effect and led to national initiatives. The effort of consolidation may provide a basis, for example, for European citizenship education.

— *It becomes easier to see where reform is necessary.* By bringing what exists together, it is apparent where a step-by-step approach to developing European citizenship has left gaps. The bundled as opposed to the unbundled approach reveals more clearly the nature of European

---

18 Eurydice. *Citizenship Education in Europe* [online]. Brussels, Education, Audiovisual and Culture Executive Agency, 2012. Available from: http://eacea.ec.europa.eu/education/eurydice/. The report is a survey of the implementation by EU-28 of the Council of Europe Charter on Education for Democratic Citizenship and human rights education.

citizenship as an unfinished and evolving status. Why for example are political rights to free movement granted in lesser order elections and not in the ones that really count - the national ones? Why are some of the channels of access and communication between the European Union and citizens voluntary and others legally binding? It also becomes clearer that reforms to involve people in the process of building Europe should not be seen in isolation but as a package of different means towards creating a European public sphere. In turn, it becomes apparent that for such reforms to work and to create a citizenship of equal opportunity, everyone should be informed, educated as a European citizen and have the opportunity to participate in a European lifelong learning programme. Whilst this might appear an ambitious agenda, practically nothing proposed would require a reform of the Treaties: it is more a question of building on and transforming what exists.[19]

- *A more holistic approach is implied by citizenship research.* A holistic rather than a scattered approach would reduce the gap between how different policy makers see European citizenship and how it is seen by scholars. "A good working definition of citizenship combines elements of rights, access and belonging".[20] A rights-only European citizenship would be a citizenship of "free riders" without responsibility and unlikely to develop further since it would lack means of access to those in power, for example, to make claims for the better development and enforcement of those rights. A participation-only citizenship would lack real substance, stripped of rights as one of its defining features. Thus in "The crisis in the European Union", Jürgen Habermas also distinguishes "three building blocks which must find embodiment in one way or another in every democratic political community."[21] He proceeds to define this as the process by which we grant each other rights, distribute power for collective decision-making and do so through "the

---

19 The exception in the attached guidelines is the proposal to change the evolutionary clause itself, Article 25 (TEFU), to make it easier to add new citizenship rights and programmes.

20 Shaw, J. *Citizenship: Contrasting Dynamics at the Interface of Integration and Constitutionalism.* European University Institute (EUI), Working Paper RSCAS 2010/60. San Domenico Di Fiesole: EUI, 2010.

21 Habermas, J. *The Crisis of the European Union: A Response.* Cambridge: Polity Press, p. 21-22, 2012.

medium of integration of civic solidarity within and across national borders." European citizenship is, of course, only a Cinderella citizenship, but it is based on elements of all three building blocks which are both present in one form or another in the European Union, but also absent in many areas, where reforms should be promoted.

In the guidelines it is suggested that this holistic approach could be agreed by the European Institutions and become legally binding. The implementation of such an approach should be the responsibility of a senior European Commissioner for European citizenship and communication. Is this a realistic demand? In the medium-term it may be to the extent that EU policy makers begin to turn to citizenship to support solutions to the internal and external challenges Europe now faces. There are also signs within the European decision-making process of a less scattered approach emerging.

In the first place, there is the idea of the "one-stop shop" where people find at least a first answer to all their questions about Europe. Whilst responsibilities for policy and enforcement of European rights remain in specialized silos Commission services have recognised that individuals often come forward with a mix of questions about residence, social rights and finding a job or recognition of their qualifications in another EU country. The response has been to work towards what is called a "cascade system" where the citizen is first informed and then advised before any remaining problems are solved. This is reflected in the setting up of Europe Direct and 800 info points across Europe, comprehensive guides on "Your Europe" and a wealth of information on the Europa website, backed up by advice and problem solving services such as Your Europe Advice (YEA) and SOLVIT. It does though take a relatively skilled and knowledgeable citizen to explore links to the assistance services.

Secondly, since the inclusion of Union citizenship in the Maastricht Treaty, there has been a trend towards more general purpose and consolidated legislation, just as the history of free movement of people started with the workers before being extended to other categories of the population. Thus Directive 2004/38 on free movement of European citizens and members of their family brings together nine separate pieces of former legislation for different categories of the population and circumstances. A similar less piecemeal approach has been developed in the area of recognition of professional qualifications, whilst the rules on co-ordination of social security entitlements now cover all categories of the population, including legally resident third country nationals. Finally, the three most recent Commission tri-annual reports on the development of Union citizenship under Article 25 TEFU have been the subject of widespread consultation, and more coordination across different departments. [22] So it is time to build a holistic European citizenship. The dilemma is that EU policy makers need a stronger sense of common citizenship now, whilst it will take at least a generation to build one. Looking ahead beyond the short-term crisis management can though encourage steps in that direction and a coming together of civil society, academics and policy makers in pursuit of such a long-term objective.

---

22 See: http://ec.europa.eu/justice/citizen/. It was thanks to a complaint by ECAS to the European ombudsman that the European Commission introduced public consultation on the citizenship report.

PART ONE:
SEARCHING FOR CINDERELLA

CHAPTER 1 How did European citizenship emerge in the context of the European Union?

Before answering this question we should recall briefly that the idea of being a citizen of Europe has much deeper historical roots than any of our family trees. The idea of being a European citizen exists independently of the European Union, but it is in that context that it has taken shape. The formal recognition of European citizenship did not just come from nowhere to be inserted in the Treaty of Maastricht a generation ago, but was the product of the work of the first generation of architects of the European Union.[23] In this chapter we show that different strands of activity led up to the Maastricht Treaty. As we have just mentioned, every three years, the Commission publishes a report on citizenship of the Union. In the third report, the Commission writes: "Citizenship of the Union is both a source of legitimisation of the process of European integration, by reinforcing the participation of citizens, and a fundamental factor in the creation among citizens of a sense of belonging to the European Union and of having a genuine European identity" (Com/2001/0506).[24] Often politicians use the term EU citizenship. However, recognition of being a European citizen comes more from identification with our continent and what we have in common, rather than from Europe as a set of institutions and rights.

European citizenship is a fragment far older than the birth of the European Union with its origin in memories passed down from classical Greece and Rome which had their own rather different versions of mutual recognition of citizenships of allied territories, or of a full transnational citizenship. After his conversion to Christianity on the road to Damascus, St. Paul could thus claim a right as a Roman citizen to be tried in Rome. The appeal of Greek democracy and the rights and freedoms enjoyed by Roman citizens were points of reference for the continuous struggle by people over centuries for freedom and democracy, with landmarks such as

---

23 For the historical perspective Willem Maas, Paul Magnette and Antje Wiener are among authors to be recommended for further reading.
24 "COM/2001/0506 final. Third Report from the Commission on Citizenship of the Union", 2001.

Magna Carta, Habeas Corpus, or the Declaration of human rights and the citizen of the French revolution. In turn, these are the inspiration for UN declarations and conventions, as well as the Council of Europe Convention on Human Rights, with its strong emphasis on post-war reconciliation and "never again". In this way, our rights as citizens do not stem only from our nation-state, but from international conventions as well.

The idea of a European space for the citizen, where peoples from friendly countries have a right without controls to visit each other's territories is also a tradition common to at least part of European society and went well before, rather than being the result of ideas of European unification. The dream of a cosmopolitan citizenship born out of this European experience can be found in many a museum or art gallery in Europe. Fortunately the Grand Tour whereby the rich, the aristocrats or the artists learned about Europe has been democratised. Particularly since the fall of the Berlin Wall and the expansion of the European Union many more young people today enjoy an experience reserved for a few in the past, a free movement right of transnational citizenship which should not be taken for granted. There is a tendency in European Union rhetoric out of deference to Member States to stress cultural diversity rather than what European culture has in common and what our citizenship has in common. The tendency is to narrow down the concept of European citizenship and link it too exclusively to the legal framework and policy making of the European Union, whereas it has in reality a much broader appeal. It would be desirable that in its rhetoric the European Union should recognise that European citizenship was not a sudden invention, but has roots in a "silent cosmopolitan revolution". A thin red line could be traced from "Civis Romanus Sum" to "Civis Europaeus Sum". How else can one explain that free movement of people is the most popular of the European Union's achievements, ahead of peace and the creation of the Euro? Could teaching of European citizenship include tracing back its historical origins? Against this background, we examine two very different historical developments – one legal and the other more political - which led to the formal inclusion of Union citizenship in the Maastricht Treaty.

(i) The European Treaties and judicial impetus towards European citizenship

If citizenship may be defined as "the right to have rights", then European citizenship did not begin with the Maastricht Treaty but with the Treaty of Rome in 1957. The intention of the negotiators was a Treaty in the mode of other efforts at post-war reconstruction, which saw the birth of the international economic institutions. The European Court of Justice went further in the landmark case Van Gend & Loos v. Netherlands Inland Revenue Administration (Case 26/62). The Court held that "the objective of the EEC Treaty which is to establish a common market the functioning of which is of direct concern to interested parties in the Community implies that this Treaty is more than an agreement which merely creates mutual obligations between the contracting states. This view is confirmed by the preamble to the Treaty which refers not only to governments but "peoples". It is also confirmed more specifically by the establishment of institutions with sovereign rights, the exercise of which effects Member States and their citizens." A reading of the spirit, not just the letter of the Treaty leads to the conclusion that European law derives something of its authority by being of the "peoples". Once Member States have conferred power on European Institutions to act, decisions and obligations resulting directly from that power can be invoked by ordinary people. "It could be said that the status of "Community citizen" had been officially recognised from the moment when the Treaties granted rights to individuals and the opportunity of enforcing them by recourse to a national or community court."[25] St. Paul could claim the right to be tried in Rome, so the EU Treaties give citizens at least the right to appeal against a failure by their own government to apply European law, an appeal which can be referred to the Court of Justice of the European Union in Luxembourg for a prejudicial ruling which is binding on the national judge and builds case-law, an official source of EU law.

The novelty of an international instrument granting rights not just to state contracting parties but also individuals should not be underestimated. This is particularly the case, because the European Court went on to fur-

---

25 Etienne Davignon, European Commissioner in the European Parliament 1979 quoted in Maas, W. *Challenges of European Citizenship*. Paper presented at the annual meeting of the American Political Science Association, Philadelhia PA, 1 September 2006.

ther strengthen the position of the citizen. In Costa v. Enel (Case C-6/64) the Court stated that "Member States have limited their sovereign rights albeit within limited fields and have thus created a body of law which binds both their nationals and themselves." Three reasons were put forward by the Court:

- The executive force of Community law cannot vary from one Member State to another because this would then undermine the objectives of the Treaty and create discrimination on the grounds of nationality which is forbidden.
- Obligations under Community law cannot be called into question by subsequent national legislation.
- The precedence of Community law is confirmed by treaty provisions that a 'regulation shall be binding' and 'directly applicable in all Member States'.

A generation later in Francovich v. Italy (Case C-479/93) the Court developed a concept of state liability to give individuals the possibility of enforcing their rights and claiming damages from their own government. In subsequent Treaty amendments, governments adopted their preferred option to enforce community law by the possibility of fines being imposed. Also, in the negotiations for the Amsterdam Treaty, care was taken in extending rights to equal treatment to ensure that a new Treaty article on prohibition of discrimination on the grounds of age, disability, race or sexual orientation had no "direct effect" which means that it could not be invoked directly by individuals in a court. Older prohibitions against discrimination on the grounds of nationality or between women and men had such a "direct effect". For every two steps forward in the cause of European citizenship, counter reactions can be expected and a step back.

It is easy to criticize such inconsistencies and overlook the vast scope of EU rules affecting our everyday lives. These remain largely unexplored and underused, particularly those resulting from European food, safety, environmental or consumer protection legislation. EU legislation – called the "*acquis communautaire*" – or 100,000 pages of rules creates standards affecting our daily life as consumers of goods or users of services. If these are not properly enforced citizens can complain to the Commission or take a case to a national court. In the guidelines on European citizenship annexed to this book, it is proposed that there should be special guides to rights in areas where EU legislation makes an impact. It is therefore a myth to suggest that European citizenship only applies to those on the move and cannot be used by sedentary citizens at home. It is the judge in one's own country who is primarily responsible for enforcing European law, referring questions if necessary to the Court of Justice of the European Union in Luxembourg. In its annual reports on the enforcement of European law, the Commission provides evidence of cases taken up on its own initiative or in response to complaints, setting great store by the role of individuals and associations acting as watchdogs to ensure that European standards are properly applied by their own government. The reach of EU law since the early judgements of the European Court has expanded significantly. The original focus was however narrow.

The idea of European rights and citizenship pre-dates the Treaty of Rome with a number of precursor initiatives and proposals such as the 1948 Hague Congress of the European Movement. At government level, only Italy had any interest in European rights because of its need to export surplus labour. This was a precondition for Italy to participate with the Benelux countries, France and Germany in the coal and steel community of 1954. Article 69 of the Treaty states that "Member States undertake to remove any restrictions based on nationality upon the employment in the coal and steel industries of workers who are nationals of Member States and have recognised qualifications." The implementation of this article was left in the hands of Member States. Ministries of Labour dragged their feet, and defined qualifications so restrictively that in the end only 300-400,000 of the Community's 1.4 million coal and steel workers qualified for the work permits which would allow them to move freely.[26]

From this first frustrating experience, it is possible that valuable lessons were learned which "may help explain the much stronger provisions of the Treaty of Rome."[27] Instead of a sectoral approach which was difficult to negotiate, the scope of free movement was extended to all workers (except for jobs in the public sector linked to the core functions of the state) who gained the right to move in the territory of the Member States, to accept offers of employment and retire there. Deadlines were set and negotiations were no longer left to Member States alone, but became the responsibility of the European Institutions with proposals initiated by the Commission. It is fashionable to read the early history of the "common market" in terms of "market citizenship" and workers as merely agents of production. That

---

26 For a detailed account of this process see: Maas, W. "The Genesis of European Rights". *JCMS: Journal of Common Market Studies,* Vol. 43, No. 5, pp. 1009-1025, 2005.

27 Ibid.

is not the impression the reader would get from the actual text of the first regulation on the free movement of workers, which goes well beyond the right to work by covering living conditions and access to services on the basis of equal treatment with workers in the host country.[28] The legislation established the right of workers and their family members to live under the same roof, to take part in trade union activity and to have access to social security and social benefits. At the time, an Italian Vice President of the European Commission Lionello Levi Sandri stated that this "represents something more important and more exciting than the free movement of a factor of production. It represents rather too an incipient form – still embryonic and imperfect – of European citizenship"[29]. Government negotiators may not have seen free movement of workers in quite such idealistic terms, but more in terms of national interest. Historically, beginning with the Italians and then the Portuguese and Spanish and more recently the countries of Central of Eastern Europe, it is those Member States which felt the negative effects of restrictions on access to the European labour market for their nationals, which have been most in favour of free movement.[30] It took a decade after the entry into force of the Treaty of Rome, for the first regulations to be adopted.

The extension of legislation for free movement of workers to the self-employed could be seen as a result of the diversification of migration flows to reflect economic change and the growth of services. The accompaniment to this was the painstaking process of drawing up legislation for the harmonisation and automatic recognition of professional qualifications, firstly profession by profession, particularly in the health sector, followed by a more general system for the mutual recognition of other qualifications which was to be less automatic.[31] In 1979, the European Commission published a draft for a directive for a general right of residence

---

28 Regulation (EEC) No 1612/68 of the Council of 15 October 1968 on freedom of movement for workers within the Community, 1968.

29 Ibid. 27.

30 With each successive enlargement of the European Union, accession agreements have given existing Member States the possibility of restricting access to the labour market for workers from new entrant countries over a transitional period, with a maximum duration of 7 years (see chapter 4).

31 Directive 2013/55/EU on the recognition of professional qualifications and Regulation (EU) No 1024/2012 on administrative cooperation through the Internal Market Information System ('the IMI Regulation'). Available from: http://eur-lex.europa.eu/LexUriServ/LexUriServ.do?uri=OJ:L:2013:354:0132:0170:en:PDF.

covering all those – students, pensioners and non-active persons – not already covered by European legislation – subject to the conditions that they have health insurance cover and "provide proof of sufficient resources to provide for their own needs and the dependent members of their family"[32]. For students proof is not required and a declaration that they have sufficient resources is sufficient. Despite support in the newly elected Parliament for this measure, there was resistance from Member States, in particular the United Kingdom and Denmark, fearing that it would lead to demands for social benefits. The Commission had to revise the package substantially and split it in three separate pieces of legislation before it was eventually adopted. This broadening of the scope of European legislation to remove barriers to free movement starting with workers in the coal and steel industries, then workers in general, the self-employed and finally the rest of the population paved the way for the Spanish proposal to introduce Union citizenship in the Maastricht Treaty.

(ii) Progress towards a peoples' Europe

If one strand in the development of Union citizenship can be traced back to judgements by the European Court of Justice and the legislation either leading to or stemming from them, another has very different origins. This second strand is reflected in initiatives for a peoples' Europe supported by Heads of State and Government in the meetings of the European Council. Concerns about a "peoples' Europe" expressed in the European Council by the European Commission and more pro-European prime ministers have not reflected any particular national interest or bargaining, but a more general concern that the process of European integration was somehow leaving the citizen behind. The European Community could lose support which in the first post war years of economic construction and growth was taken for granted and described as "latent Europeanism". This is perhaps a lesson from the past- a more benign role to which the European Council might do well to return, by paying more attention to the citizen, instead of being locked in crisis management. Whether then in a period of economic success, or now in a period of crisis, EU policy makers should

---

32 See Proposal for a Council Directive on a right of residence for nationals of Member States in the territory of another Member State 1979, OJ C207/14 and COM(79) 215 final, 26 July 1979.

recognise that the economy alone is not enough for people to identify with Europe. Student protests in 1968 marked the end of the first generation post-war period and together with the growth of the environmental movement influenced a European Council meeting in October 1972 in Paris.[33] This led to a declaration that quality of life is as important as economic growth, seeking as the European Union does now, some kind of new narrative for Europe which strikes a chord with citizens, particularly with the younger generation.

There were calls at the Paris summit to grant all Community citizens the right to vote and stand in local elections. Others, including the European Commission raised the issue that "checks at Community's internal borders should be done away with so that European citizens could become better integrated in other Member States and gradually acquire European civic rights." German Chancellor Willy Brandt observed at the summit that if "we can put social policy into a European perspective then European citizens will find it easier to identify themselves with the Community."[34] Working groups were set up on a variety of strands of activity which divided along the following lines: proposals for a passport and abolishing checks at internal borders; special rights for European citizens, including the political rights already mentioned and the values of the European Social Charter. A further strand was added to promote identification with the European community with such symbols of citizenship as a flag and an anthem.

The first attempt to bring together various initiatives for a people's Europe was a report by Leo Tindemans the Belgian Prime Minister which at the end of 1975 proclaimed the construction of Europe is not just a form of collaboration between states. [35] It is a rapprochement of people. It concluded with a statement as valid today as it was then: "the proposals for bringing Europe nearer to the citizen are directly in line with the deep

---

33 "Statement from the Paris Summit (19 to 21 October 1972)". *Bulletin of the European Communities*, No 10. , Luxembourg: Office for official publications of the European Communities, p. 14-26, October 1972.

34 Maas, W. 'The Evolution of EU Citizenship' in *Making History: European Integration and Institutional Change at Fifty. The State of the European Union,* Vol. 8. ed by Meunier, S., McNamara, K. R., Oxford: Oxford University Press, pp. 231-247, 2007.

35 Tindemans, L. "European Union: Report by Mr Leo Tindemans, Prime Minister of Belgium to the European Council". *Bulletin of the European Communities*, 1/76, 1975.

seated motivations behind the construction of Europe. They give it its social and human dimension, they attempt to restore at Union level that element of protection and control of our society which is progressively slip-
ping away from the grasp of state authority due to the nature of the problems and the internationalization of social life." He was ahead of his time
in stating the increase of power of the European Union "will make it im-
perative to ensure the rights and fundamental freedoms including economic and social rights are recognised and protected." The report also called
for the disappearance of frontier controls and a solution to the problem of
equivalence of diplomas and qualifications.

Although the report's recommendations received a frustrating reception
in the European Council they did at least start a process of consideration
over types of civic and political rights which could be granted to citizens
of Member States. The process also of implementing such recommendations was extremely slow and painful. Proof of this is that a second report
was asked for by the European Council some ten years later in June 1984.
This came from a working party chaired by a former Italian Member of
the European Parliament, Pietro Adonnino which developed the idea of
citizens' rights, the elimination of border controls and the general use of
the European passport.[36] The report led to the creation of the European
flag and the European anthem. It also made a number of proposals on cultural exchanges, youth and educational exchanges, sporting events and
volunteering.

If the impetus for these initiatives was to bring the citizens together in a
process leading to a political union and a stronger more united Europe in
foreign policy, it was also a response to periods described at the time as
"Eurosclerosis". Thus the committee chaired by Leo Tindemans declared
that "an unfinished structure does not weather well: it must be completed,
otherwise it collapses." Discussions in the European Council on a people's
Europe ran out of steam, with the new Member States, the United Kingdom, Denmark and Ireland none too supportive. Then there was a further
process of enlargement. "As Greece joined the community in 1981 and as
accession negotiations were under way with Portugal and Spain, Europe
was experiencing low economic growth coupled with high unemployment
and inflation, hardly propitious to granting new rights to "foreigners" from

---

36 Report by the Committee on a People's Europe 29 March 1985 and the report by
    the Committee on a People's Europe 28-29 June 1985 (both reports are known as
    the Adonnino Reports). Available from: http://www.ena.lu/mce.cfm.

other Member States."[37] Similar observations can be made about the more recent post-enlargement period to include thirteen new Member States after 2004.

As with free movement of workers, the lesson of history with a people's Europe appears to be "if you don't first succeed, try again" and also "change the decision-making process, making it more European and less intergovernmental". The first direct elections to the European Parliament in 1979 were a turning point, since many concerns around a people's Europe or European citizenship became politically more important. MEPs looking for issues of interest to voters found in civil society organisations advocates for enlarging the agenda of the Union in more areas of interest to people's everyday lives. The European Parliament became an advocate of Treaty reform, and for adding new areas of policy to the list of competences of the European Union. In 1984, under the leadership of Altiero Spinelli, MEP the European Parliament presented the Draft Treaty establishing the European Union (DTEU) which announced that "citizens of the Member States shall ipso facto be citizens of the Union. Citizenship of the Union shall be dependent upon citizenship of a Member State; it may not be independently acquired or forfeited. Citizens of the Union shall take part in the political life of the Union in the form laid down by the Treaty, enjoy the rights granted to them by the legal system of the Union and be subject to its laws." This was another forerunner to the Spanish proposal for Union citizenship and the mandate for negotiations leading to the Maastricht Treaty.

The year 1985 then marked a turning point from the old rhetoric towards a prospect of producing results. Building on the people's Europe report the European Commission in its white paper on completing the internal market included a section called "a new initiative in favour of community citizens", which set a timetable and deadline for the removal of obstacles to the free movement of all citizens.[38] In the Single European Act,[39]

---

37 Maas, W. "Challenges of European Citizenship". Paper presented at the 102nd annual meeting of the American Political Science Association, Philadelphia PA, 1 September 2006.

38 "Completing the internal market 1985". Available from: http://ec.europa.eu/white-papers/pdf/com85-310-internal-market_en.pdff.

39 "Single European Act 1987". Available from: http://europa.eu/eu-law/decision-making/treaties/pdf/ treaties_establishing_the_european_communities_single_european_act/treaties_establishing_the_european_communities_single_european_act_en.pdf.

which concentrated on the creation of an internal market, leaving the wider scope of the European Parliament's proposals for Treaty revision to the next revision in the Maastricht Treaty, the aim was a single market for goods, services, capital and people by 31 December 1992. That this would not be achievable for people according to that timetable was clear from another decision taken outside the European community framework in the Luxembourg town of Schengen. Five EU Member States signed an agreement to eliminate border controls, described by the Luxembourg Foreign Minister as benefitting their nationals and "moving them a step closer to what is sometimes referred to as 'European citizenship'".

Schengen is an example of an initiative taken outside the EU decision-making process and involving a smaller group of countries. In this case France, Germany and the three Benelux countries, Belgium, the Netherlands and Luxembourg, which had already eliminated border controls among themselves, became an "advance guard." Now Schengen has not only spread gradually through successive enlargements to over 26 EU and neighbouring States, it has also become incorporated in the decision-making process of the European Union. This may be a possible way forward – for example the extension of political rights attached to European citizenship might be achieved by a group of countries taking the lead. On the other hand, European citizenship should achieve the widest possible geographical scope with its potential to bring people together from an increasingly widely dispersed group of Member States. With the addition of a Europe without internal border controls to the other historical developments, the Spanish proposal for the Maastricht Treaty should not have been seen as the surprise it was at the time.

European citizenship has its origins in bottom-up judicial appeals and top-down political initiatives, which run intermittently on parallel lines. In singling out particular developments to the background to European citizenship the approach is inevitably oversimplified and may seem more logical than it was. Many of the proposals were only loosely connected together and after being made, lay dormant or were revived after long periods as attention was turned to that poor relation, the European citizen. With varying degrees of support across Member States, institutional commitment has been low, progress generally depending on a minority of committed individuals taking the lead with the decisions by the Court of Justice of the European Union as a constant source of support. In the introductions to the first three chapters in part II, we have added to the picture and brought it up to date to cover the period since the Maastricht Treaty:

- On rights, we describe how in theory European citizenship rests on a much more complete European architecture of traditional and more modern rights in the Charter and the requirement that the European Union should become a party to the Council of Europe Convention on Human Rights.
- On involvement and access to EU decision-making, developments are connected to much more recent initiatives to give the citizen a chance to connect to the European Union Institutions through access to documents and more open legislative decision-making, consultation standards, and transparency measures.
- On trust and belonging, there is a link between earlier calls for a people's Europe and the promotion of the Erasmus exchange schemes and the attempt to forge a sense of European identity.

The historical perspective shows that European citizenship is closely linked to the history of the idea of Europe and European unity and that although there was no linear planned progression a strong sense of continuity is apparent. For example it is striking how many proposals in the 1985 Adonnino report have since become reality in the various EU symbols, anniversaries and exchange programmes to strengthen European identity.[40] In the next chapter we will see that similarly there is continuity between early judgements of the Court of Justice of the European Union and its case-law after Union citizenship was introduced by the Maastricht Treaty.

---

40 McNamara, K. The Politics of everyday Europe: Constructing Authority in the European Union. Oxford: Oxford University Press, p. 62, 2015.

CHAPTER 2 How did the concept of European citizenship
progress particularly as a result of the Court of
Justice of the European Union?

The introduction of European citizenship in the Maastricht Treaty ratified in 1993 certainly aroused the interest of scholars. For some, Union citizenship was a potentially transformative concept, since for the first time a link was broken between citizenship and nationality. A transnational citizenship could therefore have a profound impact on the way we perceive citizenship *per se*. European citizenship corresponds to an ideal for Europe, which without it, is condemned to decline and increasing marginalisation in the world. At the other end of the extreme, still others saw European citizenship as sleight of hand, merely a public relations exercise, which added practically nothing to the free movement of people rights which are part of the internal market. For Richard Bellamy, for example the "four quintessentially modern commercial freedoms (people, goods, services and capital) have nothing to do with the factors which led to the establishment of liberal democracy in Member States".[41] To some extent, the lack of consensus about the meaning of European citizenship reflected the reactions to its introduction in the Treaties:

– controversy, particularly in Denmark, that Union citizenship could in some way undermine their sovereign citizenship which led to the clarification in the next Treaty revision at Amsterdam that it was additional to and in no way replaced national citizenship;

– difficulties with the introduction of the right to vote and stand in local and European elections, with again, controversy particularly in Luxembourg with its heavy concentration of European citizens, but also in France;

– concerns that European citizenship further widened the gap in rights between EU nationals and legally resident third country nationals, who were often in the same situation without enjoying equal status;

---

41 See: Bellamy, R. 'The liberty of the moderns: Market freedom and democracy within the EU.' *Global Constitutionalism,* Vol. 1, No. 1, pp. 141-172, March 2012. This is a fascinating account of such conceptual differences.

- the failure to give support to the potential and positive features of European citizenship in order to counteract such criticisms.

In reality, the most common judgement about European citizenship has been one of wait and see, and still is. At least in academic circles, there is recognition that early dismissals of European citizenship as a misguided public relations exercise and exaggerated expectations were both wrong. As in the past, it is the Court of Justice of the European Union (CJEU), which has done most to create European citizenship, so that instead of being a purely symbolic device, it has acquired legal meaning.

Article 21(1) EC contains the core rights of Union citizenship, the freedom to move and reside freely. However, it is clear from Article 21 (2) that this right is subject to 'limitations and conditions' that are laid down in the Treaty and/or in 'the measures adopted to give it effect.' The established conditions in order to exercise the free movement rights are that citizens should have sufficient resources and adequate health insurance, if they are not workers in the host country. Further, contrary to arguments that this serves as a limitation on the material scope of the Article, this is a general reservation which also exists for the other internal market freedoms. In Baumbast (Case C-413/99), the Court was clear in highlighting that although these limitations and conditions can be applied by Member States, the application is subject to judicial review by the Court, thereby providing Union citizens with a safeguard against the limitation of their rights. Further, it is established case law that limitations and conditions must be applied in compliance with the limits imposed by general principles of Community law, in particular the principle of proportionality. It was also doubted whether Article 21 was directly effective, meaning that an individual citizen of the Union can rely on this provision before the national courts. In practice the European Court has established that individual Union citizens, regardless of whether they are economically active, can rely on this article. *"The right to reside within the territory of the Member States ....conferred directly on every citizen of the Union by a clear and precise provision..."* (Baumbast). On these grounds the Court held that: *"The exercise of that right is subject to the limitations and conditions referred to in that provision, but the competent authorities and, where necessary, the national courts must ensure that those limitations and conditions are applied in compliance with the general principles of Community law and, in particular, the principle of proportionality."*

The Court "has repeatedly emphasised that Union citizenship is destined to be the fundamental status of nationals of the Member States, enabling those who find themselves in the same situation to enjoy the same treatment in law irrespective of their nationality, subject to such exceptions as are expressly provided for" (Case C-184/99) Grzelczyk was the first to state this in 2001). Not only is the "fundamental status" repeated, but it is often deliberately emphasised. For example, advocate general Sharpston stated in his opinion on the Ruiz Zambrano case (Case C-34/09) that the statement is "as important and far-reaching as those of earlier milestones in the Court's case law. Indeed, I regard the Court's description of citizenship of the Union in Grzelczyk as being potentially of similar significance to its seminal statement in Van Gend en Loos that 'the Community constitutes a new legal order of international law for the benefit of which the states have limited their sovereign rights...and the subjects of which comprise not only Member States but also their nationals'" (paragraph 68). In addition, those involved with the case-law have been intent on explaining its significance to the outside world. Hence the challenge: "'Union citizenship' has become an established term (whether one likes it or not) in Community and habitual language use, which can no longer be brushed aside, nor circumvented for reasons of personal reluctance or an allegedly better academic understanding."[42]

In his opinion on the Zambrano Case, Advocate General Sharpston set out a number of principles underpinning the approach taken by the Court: free movement as a fundamental right of citizenship, concern for children and family reunion, respect for fundamental rights and a certain degree of financial solidarity among the Member States, defining the limits of which is complex and leads to tension. In most cases described all these principles or some are applied depending on the circumstances. As the repeated statement about Union citizenship being a fundamental status indicates, the Court often reaches this conclusion by linking articles on citizenship with those on non-discrimination, (as the two concepts now are in the special title of the Lisbon Treaty). In this way on the one hand the right to move and reside freely within the territory of the Member States, subject to the limitations and conditions laid down by the Treaty and European legislation is linked on the other to the article providing a general right to equal treatment of nationals of the Member States across the whole field of the Treaty, which has a potentially broad scope. This article reads as

---

42 Dr Juliane Kokott, Advocate General, Court of Justice, Durham European Law Lecture, 2005.

follows: "*Within the scope of application of this Treaty, and without prejudice to any special provisions contained therein, any discrimination on grounds of nationality shall be prohibited.*" In terms of this article, case law has established for example that legal procedures should take place in the language of the citizens from another Member State, where that is possible, that citizens should be entitled to compensation as victims of a crime on equal terms to nationals of the Member State concerned (Case C-186/87 Cowan) and that if free admission is granted to museums for nationals of a Member State (Case C-45/93 Commission v. Spain), it is discriminatory to charge visitors from other Member States, and that there should be equal treatment on access to services at reduced rates, i.e. for students and pensioners. These are tangible benefits of European citizenship, granting equal access to services of each others' Member States.

The first case (Case C-85/96), in which the Court combined equal treatment with the notion of Union citizenship concerned Martinez Sala, an unemployed mother of Spanish nationality residing in Germany whose application for a child-raising allowance was rejected on the ground that she did not have a residence permit. Considering that the requirement to produce a residence permit constituted discrimination on grounds of nationality – as German nationals were not subject to that requirement – the Court examined whether her situation fell within the scope of application of the Treaty. In that context, the Court considered first that since the allowance was covered by Regulations No. 1612/68 and No. 1408/71, it fell within the scope of application of Community law, even if Ms. Martinez Sala herself did not fall within the scope of those regulations. The Court concluded that, irrespective of whether or not Martinez Sala qualified as a worker, she could invoke the right conferred by Article 18 EC on any citizen of the Union to move and reside freely within the territory of the Member States. Although she did not have a residence permit, she had nevertheless been authorised to reside in Germany. As a national of a Member State lawfully residing in another Member State, she came within the scope of the provisions of the Treaty on Union citizenship. The Court added that Article 17 (2) EC attaches to the status of citizen of the Union the rights and duties laid down by the Treaty, which includes the right, laid down in Article 12 EC, not to suffer discrimination on grounds of nationality. The Court held that the unequal treatment in question could not be justified and was thus forbidden by Community law.

Grzelczyk was also important as in the Court's treatment of whether a student who obviously did not qualify as a worker under Regulation

1612/68 should be entitled to a non-contributory social benefit. The Court ruled that the provisions on non-discrimination were applicable because it was the nationality of the student in this case that was the reason behind him not being able to receive the benefit, and because it had already been established in *Martinez Sala*, that Union citizens can rely on Article 12 in all situations that fall within the material scope of Community law. This particular benefit fell within the material scope of Community law on several grounds – *the introduction of citizenship of the Union,* a new chapter devoted to education and vocational training and the adoption of a relevant piece of legislation (Paragraph 35). It was held that the social benefit of job-seekers allowance falls within the scope of the Treaty or more generally may be an entitlement for Union citizens on the application of equal treatment. *"In view of the establishment of citizenship of the Union and the interpretation in the case law of the right to equal treatment enjoyed by citizens of the Union, it is no longer possible to exclude from the scope of the Treaty a benefit of a financial nature intended to facilitate access to employment in the labour market of a Member State."*

The Court was able to depart from the approach in existing case law by invoking the specific non-discrimination principle. This approach shows that the Court is willing to interpret equal treatment widely in all situations involving the exercise of the Treaty's fundamental freedoms, even though it has recently accepted more restrictions. In an earlier case, Gravier v. City of Liege (Case C-293/83), the European Court could not rely on European citizenship, which was not then in the Treaty but found that access to national training was "an indispensable element in the activities of the Community, whose objectives include inter alia the free movement, the mobility of labour and the improvement of the living standards of workers." In other words, whilst the case law of the European Court can change and some cases may even appear contradictory, it also rests on historical links, before the citizenship provisions were introduced. The European Court has nevertheless brought about a fundamental change in the perception of European citizenship by declaring that it is a status that can be relied upon purely by being a national of a Member State, irrespective of one's economic and social situation. The Court does though examine the degree of integration in the host country to take into account concerns about "benefit tourism".

The Court in the Case C-456/02 Trojani provided an explanation of the position of economically inactive citizens. The relevant question before the Court was whether this Union citizen who has a temporary right of residence, carries out 30 hours of work a week in a hostel as part of a personal reintegration programme in return for benefits to cover his basic needs i.e. whether a person who does not have sufficient resources, can enjoy a right of residence through the direct application of Article 21? The Court held in this case that in compliance with the conditions that can be applied to the exercise of the rights contained in Article 18 (1) EC, a Union citizen in these circumstances cannot derive a right from the Treaty to reside in a Member State without sufficient resources. However, the Court was able to confirm some entitlements for Mr. Trojani through holding that because of his lawful residence in Belgium, Article 12 EC prohibiting discrimination on the grounds of nationality is applicable. Therefore, he can rely on this Article to become entitled to a social assistance benefit.

In this regard it is also necessary to take note of Bidar (Case C-209/03) where the Court held that the student in this case who is economically inactive still benefits from the rights contained in the Treaty. The Court was asked whether a French student applying for a subsidised student loan in the UK could do so on equal terms to British students. Earlier cases predating Union citizenship had ruled that maintenance for students fell outside the scope of the Treaty and that therefore the provisions on non-discrimination on the grounds of nationality could not apply (Lair and Brown). The Court recalled its ruling in Trojani according to which, with regard to social assistance benefits, a citizen of the Union who is not economically active may rely on the provision on equal treatment, where he has been lawfully resident for a certain period of time or holds a residence permit. In fact he had been living in the UK for some years apparently with sufficient resources and sickness insurance. Access to student loans was however limited to persons "settled". The Court accepted that a three year's residence requirement was fair but that the conditions attached to "settled" were too strict and discriminated against nationals of other Member States.

The Court does not refrain from requiring Member States to extend certain benefits to European citizens whilst its case law also reflects a genuine concern not to distort the solidarity mechanism of national social assistance systems. For example in the case concerning Elisabeta Dano (Case C-333/13), the Court ruled that a Member State must have the possibility of refusing to grant social benefits to economically inactive Union citizens who exercise their right to freedom of movement solely in order to obtain another state's social assistance. The Court considered that the plaintiff showed no intention of finding work. The Member States are expected to accept a certain degree of financial solidarity between their citizens and those of other Member States, particularly if the latter are connected for a certain period of time, need to overcome temporary difficulties, and are not deliberately using their freedom of movement to claim assistance as "benefit tourists." This has implications for European policy making in the legislative, but perhaps more importantly in the non-legislative area, and the possible use of the European social fund as a way of overcoming tensions between free movement rights and Member States' protection of their social assistance budgets. The European Court recognises that Member States have a right to reserve some specific benefits to European citizens from other Member States that show a sufficient degree of integration in their society and exclude others. This often makes it difficult for example to follow the logic of the case-law. Is there a contradiction for example between the Martinez Sala and Elisabeta Dano cases? Is the CJEU becoming more cautious in its defence of European citizenship and more attentive to Member States' concerns about benefit tourism?

An interesting area of difficulty in reconciling free movement rights with the prerogatives of Member States concerns the parents' right to choose names for their children, in conformity with their own identity and traditions. In case C-148/02 Garcia Avello v. Belgium, the facts were as follows:

> "*Carlos Garcia Avello, a Spanish national, and his wife Isabelle Weber, a Belgian national, had two children of dual nationality, born In Belgium. In accordance with Belgian law and practice, the children were given the surname 'Garcia Avello' on their birth certificate. In accordance with Spanish law and practice, the children had, however also been registered with the Spanish Embassy in Brussels under the surname 'Garcia Weber'. A few years later, the parents asked the Belgian authorities to change their children's surnames to 'Garcia Weber', contending that the Spanish system of surnames was deeply rooted in Spanish law, tradition and custom to which the children felt more intimately related. Furthermore, the name 'Garcia Avello' suggested under that system that they were siblings rather than children of their father and deprived them of any link in name to their mother. A change would enable them to use the same name in Belgium and Spain; it was not likely to cause harm to anyone else or give rise to confusion, and the fact that they would keep the element Garcia would guarantee continuity of name in the pa-*

*ternal line. Though the Belgian law permitted change in certain circum-
stances, the application was rejected."* [43]

In his opinion, the Advocate General noted that the refusal to change the name affected not only the father but also the children's interest, and that this was not a wholly internal situation since the father had exercised his free movement rights and the children have Spanish nationality as well. The Court ruled that the principle of non-discrimination, precluded refusal to grant the children to bear the surname to which they are entitled according to the law and tradition of the second Member State. Such cases illustrate in a very practical way core issues of European identity, which tends to be a general and abstract debate. Differences in name for different children and members of the family do give rise to difficulties when airlines, banks or migration officials make identity checks.

Another case, which also illustrates the importance attached by the Court to children and the family concerns the very high profile "baby Chen" (Case C-200/02). A Chinese couple went to Ireland for the birth of their second child (thus circumventing Chinese one-child policy) where the child simply by being born on the island of Ireland acquired Irish nationality and therefore European citizenship. The case arose because Sue Chen's mother wished to move to the UK. The UK argued that this was simply an attempt to 'exploit' European law by giving birth to a child in a way to acquire European citizenship. The European Court of Justice responded by reasoning that Irish law determining nationality must be respected. As a member of the family of an EU citizen, and as her carer, Mrs Chen was held by the Court to have the right to reside in the UK. Recourse to European law may well have placed the family in a more advantageous position, than if they had sought to rely on immigration rules, to which this case was seen as a challenge. A number of copy-cat baby Chen cases followed. Ireland subsequently altered its constitution, limiting the granting of birth right citizenship to children of its own citizens or those otherwise entitled to be citizens. Another case which illustrated the readiness of the Court to challenge the Member States on the sensitive terrain of immigration law concerned the interpretation by Ireland of the provision of the so-called "citizenship" directive (2004/38). Ireland wished to

---

43 As described by Francis Jacobs, the advocate General in this case in "Citizenship of the European Union – A legal analysis", *European Law Journal*, 13(5), pp. 591-610, *September 2007.*

restrict the right of residence on its territory to spouses or partners of European citizens from third countries to those who had been previously lawfully resident in another Member State. In reality, the Court found that there is no such requirement in the "citizenship directive" (Case C-127/08 Metock and others).

The more recent Ruiz Zambrano case (Case C-34/09) can be considered as building on the two previous examples and as having more far-reaching implications. The case concerned a Colombian citizen who claimed asylum in Belgium along with his wife and first child. The authorities refused asylum, but did not order their return. The family remained and integrated with the birth of two further children, who acquired dual citizenship. When in 2005 Mr Zambrano applied for welfare benefit, his irregular situation and lack of a work permit came to the attention of the authorities, which ordered the deportation of the parents. This, it was argued, would have deprived the right of the children to residence in the EU as European citizens, even though they had never exercised their free movement rights. The case is a clear endorsement of a rights-status connection for EU citizenship. This status can override national immigration law, as pointed out in a detailed criticism (Hailbronner 2013). The Court concluded that "Article 20 TFEU precludes national measures which have the effect of depriving citizens of the Union of the genuine enjoyment of the substance of the rights conferred by virtue of their status as citizens of the Union." In the case of the Zambrano children, a right connected to this status to remain in Belgium and possibly at some future date to move to other EU countries – a theoretical, future rather than an actual situation – was upheld. Immediately after Zambrano, the Court was less sympathetic in the case of Mrs McCarthy (Case C-434/09), and would not accept that she was being deprived of her EU citizenship rights which she had not used, her situation being assessed as entirely internal. There are therefore self-imposed limits to the reach of the Court especially when the use of the rights triggered by European citizenship is hypothetical rather than real.

In March 2010, the CJEU reached a judgement concerning the acquisition and loss of nationality itself and its relationship to European citizenship (Case C-135/08 Rottman v. Freistaat Bayern). Dr. Janko Rottmann an Austrian citizen was prosecuted for alleged fraud and moved to Germany, where he sought naturalisation. As a result he automatically lost his Austrian citizenship, but when the German authorities found out about his past, they took the decision to revoke naturalisation on the grounds that it had been obtained fraudulently. The European court rejected the idea that this was an entirely internal situation, since Mr. Rottmann, as a result of these events, was in a position capable of becoming stateless and therefore losing his Union citizenship. By reason of its nature and consequences, the case fell within the ambit of European law (paragraph 42). The Court went on to assure the Member States that "the legitimacy, in principle, of a decision withdrawing naturalisation on account of a deception, remain in theory, valid when the person in question loses, in addition to the Member State of naturalisation, citizenship of the Union" (paragraph 14). Nonetheless, the Court empowered the national court "to ascertain whether the withdrawal decision at issue...observes the principle of proportionality, so far as concerns the consequences it entails for the situation of the person concerned in the light of European law."

In a debate on the question "has the European Court of Justice challenged Member State sovereignty in nationality law?" conducted by the EUDO observatory on citizenship, opinions among academics appeared to differ as to the significance of this judgement.[44] The answer to the question appears in general to be, with some regrets, that the CJEU did not take the opportunity of this case to take a more principled stand and assert the autonomous nature of European citizenship. In reality the Court built on earlier cases and in particular Micheletti (Case C-369/90) which confirmed that determination of nationality falls within the exclusive competence of the Member States, but that this competence must be exercised with due regard to the requirements of EU law.

The Rottmann judgement does not assert a European citizenship of a cosmopolitan type somehow independent from national citizenship. It does though reiterate its "fundamental status" and assert that it is more than just an automatic tributary of national citizenship. The case offers guidance to national courts and legislative and administrative authorities as to what an EU standard of proportionality might demand in the loss and potentially the acquisition of citizenship. In Rottmann and in other more recent cases where there is not necessarily a link between Union citizenship and equal treatment, the European Court has shortened and in a way strengthened its doctrinal stance and simply repeated that Union citizenship "is destined to be the fundamental status of the nationals of the Member States."

---

44 See Shaw, J. "Has the European Court of Justice challenged Member State sovereignty in nationality law?" EUI Working Papers, RSCAS 2011/62, EUDO Citizenship Observatory, European University Institute, 2011.

In looking back over the cases of the CJEU, it is surprising that they have not led the European Commission to take more initiatives to bring their significance to the attention of ordinary people, companies and Member States' authorities. It is surprising too that decisions by the European Court do not receive more media attention. Where the case-law has had more influence has been on secondary legislation, and in particular the citizenship directive (Directive 2004/38) discussed later. In areas of more economic importance such as the free movement of goods, the European Commission has not hesitated to draw conclusions and issue guidelines for Member States. One reason for the Commission's hesitation may be the very tensions between the Court's decisions and national prerogatives. Once the Court established that European citizenship was a basis on which demands for judicial review could be made, and once it became detached from its economic origins, outcomes were bound to be unpredictable. These demands will increase and the binding nature of the Charter of Fundamental Rights will encourage them further. The decisions by the Court are situated in areas which relate to the difficult determination of the place of Union citizenship in relation to national citizenship. The cases touch on a wide range of policies which are of primary importance in both political and budgetary terms: access to social benefits, student grants and loans, vocational training schemes. They also touch on areas which may not have financial consequences but which are extremely sensitive in terms of national sovereignty, such as issues of personal identity and citizenship. Also, running through the cases is the theme of tension between European citizenship and free movement within the Union and international migration.

Much of the case law leaves open many questions as to what its real practical implications may be. Often unusual circumstances are involved, unlikely to reoccur frequently (see Rottman). Nevertheless, it is clear that Union citizenship has evolved from its market origins. From the proposals by the Spanish government in May 1990 which led to the inclusion of citizenship in the Maastricht Treaty, the idea was to transform a space which was essentially economic designed to guarantee free movement into an integrated common European space where the citizen could play the main role, in a political union. The European Court points the way forward. The result is that European citizens have more rights than they think they have. It is not for citizens to justify their presence anywhere in the Union, but for the Member States to justify that any restriction on the use of a vast area of freedom and opportunity should be proportionate and justified in the public interest.

The case law of the European Court by no means proposes open-ended solidarity among Member States, or automatic access to assistance. European free movement is not comparable to the United States where it would be unthinkable to impose restrictions on people on the move, on the grounds that they have insufficient resources to support themselves. This is because the US has federal programmes for disadvantaged and handicapped people and the States of the Union are deemed to sink or swim together. Maybe in the EU (as recommended in chapter five), there should at least be a programme for emergency assistance, so that European citizens falling through all the safety nets receive some support from a European fund rather than placing all the burden on the host country. Whilst recognition that Member States have to protect their system against abuse, and can impose certain conditions such as a degree of integration and evidence of residence, the case law of the CJEU sets limits on those conditions. This needs to be born in mind when we consider in the next chapter pressures by Member States to restrict so-called benefits tourists' access to health care and social services.

CHAPTER 3 European rights to free movement: both extensively practiced and controversial

In the aftermath of the 2008 financial crisis, politicians are focusing inevitably not so much on free movement of citizens as free movement of workers. In this chapter we reflect the debate on the need to create a European labour market and the tensions round that concept. At the same time we point to the danger of focusing too much on employment alone and overlooking a much broader range of mobility practice and therefore the full range of policy implications involved. The "freedom to travel, study and work anywhere in the EU" is the leading representation associated with the European Union, being mentioned by 49% of the population (Eurobarometer 83-2015). European rights to free movement are among the most popular of the European Union's achievements with 57% of people sharing this view according to a Eurobarometer poll, and a majority also believing that it is good for their own economy.[45] An internal market of four interlinked freedoms of people, goods, services and capital is the basis on which the European Treaties, legislation and policies are built. Moreover, the right to move freely around Europe is the first right of European citizenship. For the young generation, Europe, a space of freedom stretching from Edinburgh to Zagreb, Lisbon to Riga, is taken for granted, but it is also a legacy which has to be defended. Economic studies all point towards similar conclusions: with an ageing population, Europe requires more, not less free movement of workers. This is also needed to absorb asymmetric shocks between the periphery and core Euro zone countries. Free movement in aggregate is seen as a win-win situation for European migrants themselves, countries of origin, and host countries. Newcomers fill vacancies which are complementary rather than competing with the domestic workforce. Mobile workers contribute more in taxes than they receive in benefits.

Why then has free movement of people within the Union become a contentious issue as shown for example during the campaign for elections to

---

45 See for example standard Euro barometer no. 365 of February 2013.

the European Parliament in May 2014 and in the run up to the UK referendum on membership of the EU? A number of reasons can be put forward:

- The economic and monetary crisis has brought to the surface tensions between national and European citizenship, expressed in the rise of eurosceptical parties. Centrifugal forces and fragmentation are on the rise.
- Before the 2004 and 2007 enlargements, free movement of people within the European Union was not an issue. Arguments over "transitional arrangements" and restrictions on access to the labour market raised fears of competition for jobs and undercutting of wages in host countries and a sense of being treated as second class citizens for people moving from the new Member States. The seeds were sown for free movement to become more controversial. After 2004 the 15 old Member States were joined first by 10 new Member States including eight from central and Eastern Europe (known as the A8 workers rather than European citizens), Cyprus and Malta followed by Bulgaria and Romania in 2007 and then Croatia in 2013.
- Whilst the overall picture remains, despite enlargement from 15 to 28 Member States, of a low-level of free movement within the EU by comparison with other parts of the world, local perceptions and facts can contradict the aggregate figures. Free movement remains unevenly spread and heavily concentrated on certain trajectories and destinations. Local problems with vulnerable European citizens and strain on local services were insufficiently anticipated by EU and national policy-makers.
- There has been a failure of political discourse with even mainstream parties allowing free movement of people within the EU to become associated with an increasingly toxic debate about immigration and the perceived failure of migration policies.
- In this debate, free movement of people tends to be presented as if it were an absolute freedom, even though complaints show it is fraught with obstacles. European citizens are under an obligation to have comprehensive health insurance and sufficient resources not to be a burden on the host Member State. Benefit tourism is more myth than reality.

The purpose of this chapter is to explore the arguments about how to defend European free movement as fundamental both to European citizenship and the very existence of the European Union. The role of the Commission as guardian of the Treaties in enforcing rights to free movement is essential. Citizens too should play a more active role. Can European citizens' rights be entrusted to the European Institutions and ultimately national governments which are the masters of the Treaties? Are not trade-offs always possible?

(i) Patterns of free movement of people

Europe is on the move, certainly to a greater extent than the official statistics suggest with intra-EU migration taking on increasingly diverse forms. According to the official statistics (Eurostat), 13.5 million European citizens were residing in another Member State in 2013, less than the 21 million third country nationals in the EU.[46] The immediate onslaught of the economic crisis brought about a slow-down in intra-EU free movement, but it very quickly picked up and increased, taking a larger share of migratory flows as a whole. For young people in the hardest hit countries in the Euro zone, the possibility to find jobs in Germany and other better performing economies is a tangible benefit of European citizenship, although South to North movements remain well below those from "new" to "old" Member States. The official statistics do not capture all forms of mobility, such as seasonal or posted workers on temporary assignments in another Member State or cross-border commuting between place of residence and place of work or the more recent trend to long-distance commuting. Such impermanent forms of mobility could add a further 2.5 million to the total of 13.5 million. There are more significant but unknown numbers of European citizens whose movements go unrecorded because they stay for a short period, but who are effectively resident in two Member States. Job-seekers who cannot rely on unemployment benefits are largely off the radar screen as well. "Migration as a phenomenon presents formidable problems in terms of statistical measurements".[47]

Whilst the political importance attached to free movement of people is leading to increasing numbers of studies, improving knowledge of what is

---

46 Eurostat. "EU citizenship - statistics on cross-border activities". April 2013. Available from: http://ec.europa.eu/eurostat/statistics-explained/index.php/EU_citizenship_-_statistics_on_cross-border_activities#Foreign.C2.A0population_in_the_EU_and_Member_States.

47 Riso, S. S., Olivier, J. E., Andersen, T. *Labour migration in the EU: Recent trends and policies*. Eurofound, Publications Office of the European Union: Luxembourg, 2014.

really happening, particularly at the local level, for reasons we explain later, is a priority.[48] According to a special Eurobarometer poll on geographical mobility, 10% of Europeans have experience of living for a time in another Member State. Different forms of regular transnational mobility and networking, including "virtual", may be practiced by 30% of 508 million inhabitants of the EU, so that sociological Europe is much bigger than the Europe to create a single European labour market and very different from political Europe.[49] Is this not positive news for Europe? Civil society organisations, professional bodies and associations of communities living abroad such as Europeans throughout the world (ETTW) have a role in drawing attention to mobility as not just employment related but involving a much broader range of practices and therefore policies across the board, and a more holistic European citizenship approach.

Mobility is more widespread than officially recognised. It also covers all possible choices of occupation and income disparities from the top to the bottom of the scale. At the risk of caricature this should lead policy makers to take into account a heterogeneous population across a wide range of policies.

- *Euro-workers* are the original foot soldiers of Europe, surplus labour from the South needed in the heavy industry sectors of the North. Their successors are the construction and other low or semi-skilled workers from the countries of Central and Eastern Europe, often working below their level of qualifications. Whilst governments tend to stress the value of high-skilled Euro-migrants, in reality low-skilled work can contribute just as much to economic growth.
- *Euro-entrepreneurs* are those who are targeted by the rules on right of establishment for the professions, internal market rules such as the services directive, or measures to reduce the time and administrative burden it may take to set up a business in another Member State. Maybe they have succeeded in filling a niche market at home, so why not ex-

---

48 This chapter draws on work by Dhéret, C., Lazarowicz, A., Nicoli, F., Pascouau, Y., Zuleeg, F. *Making progress towards the completion of the single European labour.* EPC Issue Paper no. 75, European Policy Centre, May 2013.

49 See: Recchi, E. et al. *The Europeanisation of Everyday Life: Cross-Border Practices and Transnational Identities among EU and Third-Country Citizens. Final Report.* EUCROSS, June 2014.
European Commission. *New Europeans.* Special Eurobarometer. April 2011. Available from: http://ec.europa.eu/public_opinion/archives/ebs/ebs_346_en.pdf.

pand and try the formula elsewhere in Europe? Euro-entrepreneurs often have complex questions about short or long-distance commuting, tax, social security, and family members' rights – a mix of personal and professional preoccupations.

– *Euro-lovers* have attracted the attention of researchers.[50] The practice of free movement and the choice of where to live and work in another country may not be influenced by economic factors or even professional development alone, but also by the difficulty of managing a relationship at a distance with long periods of absence. If the Euro-lovers stay together and found a family, their choice of which languages to use at home, how the children are brought up, whether they access the media of the host country, or the countries of origin, all such factors make this citizenship group an interesting laboratory for the study of European identity.

– *Euro-learners* are an increasingly important category with growing awareness that a period studying in another EU Member State or outside the EU "looks good" on a *Curriculum vitae*. Students are aware of the difference in performance of universities across Europe. A period studying abroad may be time out, and a relatively easy option for some, or more essential for others, to make up for deficiencies in education at home and learn another language (in particular – English). The Erasmus scheme is seen as one of the EU's success stories. The main problem is that the chance to study abroad tends to be given to high achieving students likely to have such opportunities in any case, whereas research suggests that for less well off or educated students, having such an opportunity is particularly appreciated and productive.

– *Euro-sun seekers* tend to be pensioners from the North seeking a better climate for their retirement on the shores of the Mediterranean or Adriatic. Often they bring with them their own services, native language media and expat associations, whilst complaining about their own lack of integration in their adopted country of residence. Within the Euro zone, the risks of currency fluctuations to one's pension or the value of one's property are reduced, but the crisis has signalled new risks. It has also created new opportunities for pensioners to buy property at re-

---

50 Professor Robert Miller, Queen University, Belfast is coordinator of a research project on the evolution of European identity in private life. See: www.euroidentities.org.

duced prices in Greece, Spain or Portugal. Euro-sun seekers are also taking advantage of the crisis.

– *Euro-stars* are among the young people whose parents and grandparents may have been Euro-lovers or Euro something else. They regard themselves as European citizens, finding that attachment to more than one country and a readiness to move, work in different languages comes naturally. Many came out of the period when Erasmus was a novelty and had a more formative influence. Euro-stars are well qualified, linguistically competent, involved with each other through developing extensive transnational networks and likely to be politically active. They are strongly attracted to civic activism beyond the nation state.[51]

And finally there are the Euro-tourists who are by far the largest category bringing with them their own distinct concerns over travel documents, car rental, roaming charges, health and safety....

(ii) Costs and benefits of labour mobility

The benefits of more rather than less freedom of movement in the European Union are argued by a significant volume of European but also national studies, which were well summed up and brought together in a lecture by a former member of the European Commission: "EU migrant workers can help the host country's economy to function better by addressing skills shortages and labour market bottlenecks. They contribute to macroeconomic demand and to government revenues, so they can help to create more jobs in the host country. They can also help to reduce the tax burden on the domestic population."[52] This is not therefore a zero sum game. The same lecture goes on: "all available studies point in the same direction. There is a consensus among experts on these fundamental, overall advantages of EU labour mobility." An additional argument and one which leads many studies to conclude that the level of labour mobility in

---

51 Frevert, U. 'How to become a good European citizen: present challenges and past experiences.' in Georgi, V. B. (ed.) *The Making of Citizens in Europe: New Perspectives on Citizenship Education,* pp. 37-51, Bonn: Bundeszentrale fur politische Bildung, 2008.

52 Speech by Laszlo Andor titled "Labour Mobility – The inconvenient truth." Lecture at Bristol University, 10 February 2011.

Europe is low, for example by comparison with the US, is that "it is also a necessity to make the European monetary union (EMU) more resilient."[53] "Free movement of workers within the EU does not appear to be acting as a significant shock absorber against the widening economic asymmetries between core and periphery within the EU."[54] In theory, free movement is a win-win situation: well prepared migrant workers can improve their living standards and gain additional skills and competencies; host countries gain because they are more likely to be of working age on average than the local population, and therefore, less likely to claim benefits whilst countries of origin can receive remittances and the return of more skilled workers, if their period abroad in the EU is temporary rather than permanent. Whilst the bigger picture is one where the benefits of labour mobility outweigh the costs – it is always possible to find specific examples where this aggregate positive scenario is contradicted by specific facts on the ground. The challenge for policy makers is to address these specific concerns and not fall in the trap of accepting that they are in any way typical of the overall situation and then giving way to demands for general restrictions. "Member States' governments should address these genuine concerns by tackling the specific problems – and not by restrictions on their free movement."[55] Let us look now at the motives for free movement, concerns about its abuse and its impact on local services.

The main pull factors are the availability of jobs and people move to work or look for work not to access social benefits. They therefore compare wages and the cost of living in their own country and a possible new country of residence. This decision-making process does not though necessarily follow just the economic logic necessary to create a well-functioning European labour market. Other factors come in play, such as social networks, linguistic and cultural ties with "some empirical evidence, migration flows between countries with closely related languages tend to be larger than between countries with unrelated languages."[56]

Given the uneven performance in Europe in language skills, proposals to improve the functioning of the European labour market place emphasis on giving more support to intra-EU migrants to learn the language of the

---

53 Ibid. 48.
54 Ibid.
55 Ibid. 53.
56 Belot, M., Ederveen, S. "Cultural and institutional barriers in migration between OECD countries", Mimeo, 2006.

country of destination. There is also increasing recognition that family and social ties are a deterrent, explaining the gap between theoretical intentions to move and actually doing so.[57] Migration flows may be encouraged by transnational networks or they may be discouraged by the loss of social capital in one's country of origin which is difficult to replace in one's country of destination. Studies of how to improve the functioning of the European labour market place emphasis on the need for mentoring and personalised guidance and on upgrading EURES (European employment services). Given the wide variety and heterogeneous categories of people on the move, policy makers need to address issues outside the labour market, and work more closely with associations representing European citizens and providing them with information and advice about working and living conditions abroad.

In chapter 5, a number of proposals are put forward to reduce the gaps between the fine principles of European law and the practice on the ground by national administrations, which tend to stress the exceptions rather than the spirit of European law. Most advice services will confirm that more people are coming to their doors with more serious complaints. It is difficult to conclude whether this is due to a hardening of attitude towards EU citizens by front-line officials, or increased awareness by citizens of their rights. The barriers are well known: obstacles to free movement and residence, particularly for EU families including third country nationals; risks of expulsion of low income job-seekers; delays in accessing social entitlements or recognition of professional qualifications and the volume of papers and "red tape" due to the failure of Member States to recognise each other's documents. Increased public awareness of the barriers to free movement within Europe and the failure to eliminate them, could lead many more people to seek work outside Europe.

As the Eurofound study puts: "It is clear that the national debate in many countries has increasingly focussed on the negative rather than the positive prospects of intra-EU mobility."[58] In this debate, the barriers to intra-EU mobility are ignored. Free movement is seen as an absolute and unconditional freedom, which is being abused. The European Commission has on repeated occasions demanded evidence of abuse but "no Member

---

57 20% of European citizens are interested to move but only 1.2% have a firm intention to do so (presentation by Jorg Tanner European Commission to EESC conference of 27 January 2015).

58 Ibid. 48.

State has given the Commission any factual evidence that so-called benefit tourism is systematic or widespread."[59] In a communication "Free movement of EU citizens and their families: Five actions to make a difference" (COM (2013)837 final of 25.11.2013), the Commission spells out the rights and obligations attached to free movement and aims to address the concerns raised by some Member States by helping them to fight marriages of convenience and apply EU social security coordination rules or meet the challenges of social inclusion. [60] Whilst there is little evidence of "benefit tourism" as a push factor for intra-EU migration, there are circumstances in which reliance on benefits may be a reason to stay in the country, rather than return home. This can occur for example when free movement is abused by unscrupulous employers paying EU migrants less than the minimum wage, and exploiting them in other ways by imposing illegal contract conditions, housing and other costs, so that the experience of free movement ends in failure. Nevertheless the extent of reliance on benefits is greatly exaggerated.

More serious concerns relate to strains on local services in countries of destination and brain drain in countries of origin. In the communication "Five actions to make a difference" the Commission mentions for the first time "efforts to help build the capacity of local authorities to use European structural and investment funds efficiently". The message is therefore that the overall benefits of free movement of people and the rights attached to them should be preserved, but that more than just the EU regulatory framework is required to deal with problems on the ground. In a report to the Commission with recommendations for the future of cohesion policy 2014-2020, (the so-called Barca report) it was argued that "cohesion policy, by combining EU principles and the freedom of member states and regions as well as local institutions to apply them to specific needs, could serve as the appropriate framework to take one step further."[61] Migration is recommended as one of priorities for the funds. The report argues that

---

59 Ibid. 53.
60 The UK, Germany, Austria and the Netherlands raised such concerns in a joint letter to the Irish Presidency. This communication provides valuable guidance with its reference to the Treaties, European legislation, and a number of opinion polls and studies, including one by ICF GHK milieu: A fact-finding analysis on the impact on the Member States' social security systems of the entitlements on non-active intra-EU migrants to special non-contributory cash benefits and health care.
61 Barca, F. *An agenda for reformed cohesion policy: A place-based approach to meeting European Union challenges and expectations,* 2009.

"citizenship is de facto defined in part by the accessibility of people to services" – from which it follows that European citizenship is about access to each others' services, to mutual advantage. Therefore, "an EU place-based approach can respond to the highly differentiated way in which migration inflows and outflows affect different places." [62] The more recent influx of asylum seekers and immigrants simply serves to show how right this report was to recommend migration as one of the priorities for the EU social and regional funds.

Because patterns of free movement are so strikingly uneven across the member states, there are regions and cities in countries of destination where strains on local services – housing, health, schooling, transport - can be affected by the sudden and unexpected arrival of a large number of newcomers. Migration can become also a convenient scapegoat for cuts in public services and failure to invest in local infrastructure. This is an area of policy to be addressed therefore on the basis of sound local population statistics and economic evidence. Similarly, problems of brain drain and the loss of skilled workers to maintain the infrastructure in specific regions of countries of origin are equally real. Matching supply and demand across borders in health services may be to mutual advantage but it does not always work that way, if it has negative repercussions and leads to staff shortages in such services in left behind regions.

For many of the recommendations to improve European policy on free movement of people, cohesion policy is the right context. The social fund can address issues of training for mobility and social inclusion: the regional fund could be used to help meet infrastructure development needs of localities in countries of origin and countries of destination. The proposal in chapter 5 is that the two should be linked in a European free movement solidarity fund, which can be set up as part of EU cohesion policy using existing resources. This is also the framework within which exchange of best practice can be encouraged and successful local experiments can be spread to tackle the unwarranted side effects from the benefit of free movement. Although the economy gains from the new arrivals, it is important to demonstrate to the domestic sedentary population that they should not bear the full cost in increased demand for public services, but that this should be shared between countries of origin, countries of destination and the EU budget – a much fairer deal. Moreover, within the struc-

---

62 Ibid.

tural funds, the principle of partnership for local community development and its delivery by local action groups has been strengthened. Such projects can be introduced now in both rural and urban areas. As the Barca report recommended, migration and free movement of people should become a priority. This ought to be reflected in the new cycle of EU cohesion funds which will begin in 2020.

(iii) Combatting scaremongering about free movement of persons

At a conference to celebrate the 25th anniversary of the European Foundation Centre (EFC), considerable attention was given to the issue of migration.[63] Should the discourse of migration be changed? The consensus appeared to be that actions speak louder than words, to answer peoples' concerns. As the examples below show, it is from a narrative about a specific issue to do with borders, a group in the population, or locality, that below the surface of the apparent popularity of EU free movement, hostility can be stirred up. This is being done, as the campaign for the 2014 European elections showed, not only by eurosceptical or fringe parties, but by mainstream politicians as well. In all the examples below, the populist conclusion would be restrictions on free movement, and even the reinstatement of border controls. The response should be to resist such restrictions and make free movement work better. Without such a response, scaremongering about free movement has considerable resonance.

The Polish plumber

In France, in the run-up to the 2005 referendum, which saw the rejection of the Constitutional Treaty, "the Polish plumber" became a celebrity. This mythical example was derived from the first version of the EU services directive, which proved highly controversial. Based on the costs of labour being on average 3.47€ per her hour in the new Member States and 22.19€ per hour in EU 15, the Polish plumber is able to offer his services

---

63 EuroPhilantopics, 4-5 November 2014. See: http://www.efc.be/newsevents/ europhilantopics/.

in Paris from Poland, driving his French competitors out of business.[64] Business leaders and the "yes" campaign pointed to the shortage of plumbers in Paris, whilst a Polish travel agency produced a poster of a plumber as a male sex symbol with the slogan: "I am staying in Poland."

The "Roma affair"

Again in France, but also in Italy and to a more limited extent in other EU member states, the rights of Roma as European citizens was a further test of legislation and policy on free movement of people. The dismantling of Roma camps over the summer of 2010 by the Sarkozy government, combined with the repatriation of the inhabitants eventually led to mass expulsion, which is forbidden by the Citizenship Directive and the Charter of Fundamental Rights.[65] The European Roma Rights Centre in Budapest[66], civil society organisations in Paris, Bucharest and Brussels took up the cause, but whilst their legal arguments were sound, the basis in terms of evidence and the willingness of those directly affected to step forward was weak. In the discussion between the delegation for the Commission and the French government, the European citizens concerned needed to be – if not physically present – at least there as a third party. The problems found by the Commission in enforcing European legislation and the Charter directly in an emergency situation were evident. This explains why Viviane Reding, the Commissioner responsible, used political rather than legal pressure, stating that Europe had not seen such deportations since the Second World War.

---

64 A more real case is the Laval judgment of the European Court of Justice involving the use of Latvian posted workers to build a school across the border in Sweden below the rates agreed in collective bargaining between Unions and employers in that region. Case C-341/05.

65 For an in-depth analysis see Carrera S. 'The Framing of the Roma as Abnormal EU Citizens: Assessing European Politics on Roma Evictions and Expulsions in France' in: E. Guild (ed.) *The Reconceptualization of European Union Citizenship*, pp. 33–63. Leiden: Brill Nijhoff, 2014.

66 European Roma Rights Centre (ERRC) is a public interest law organisation focused on fighting anti-Roma discrimination. See: http://www.errc.org/.

Political exploitation of tensions over open borders

Tensions over Schengen appeared at intervals to be signalling a spillover from the Euro crisis affecting Europe's achievements in guaranteeing open borders. There was a Dutch proposal to monitor border crossings and a Danish proposal to strengthen border controls towards Sweden and Germany. This was despite the long tradition of absence of border controls in the countries of the Nordic Council. A more serious dispute between France and Italy over refugees from Libya was referred by Silvio Berlusconi and Nicolas Sarkozy to the European Council, which meeting in June 2011 asked for legislative proposals. The aim was to extend the Schengen safeguard clause so that as a measure "of very last resort" it would "allow the exceptional reintroduction of internal border controls in a truly critical situation", meaning where a Member State was no longer in control of immigration on its external Schengen frontiers. The legislation has been adopted since.[67] The problem with this measure is that it reduces the pressure on all Schengen states to maintain free movement of persons within the Schengen zone and agree on common asylum and immigration policies.

The Commission defended this proposal as a lesser of two evils, and a way to contain strain to the Schengen system, whilst at the same time, demanding more European supervision of the safeguard clause. The attacks on Schengen have withstood the economic and financial crisis as well as anti-immigration rhetoric. The newly-won freedom to travel across the European continent since the fall of the Berlin wall and the extension of the Schengen zone to the new Member States (except Bulgaria and Romania) can no longer be taken for granted however. New calls were made to review Schengen and reinstate national border controls during summer 2015 in response to the refugee crisis. In early 2016 such pressure became more intense creating doubts about the survival of Schengen.

---

67 Regulation (EU) No 1051/2013 of the European Parliament and of the Council of 22 October 2013 amending Regulation (EC) No 562/2006 in order to provide for common rules on the temporary reintroduction of border control at internal borders in exceptional circumstances [online]. *Official Journal of the European Union,* L 295/1, 2013.

Popular initiative in Switzerland in favour of immigration quotas

By a wafer thin majority, 50.3% of the Swiss population voted on 9 February 2014 in favour of an initiative by the right wing People's Party. The new constitutional provision approved in the referendum provides that "the number of permits entitling foreigners to reside in Switzerland shall be subject to annual ceilings and quotas." The promoters of the initiative distanced themselves from more extreme supporters such as the Egerkingen Committee, which co-ordinated the successful campaign for the proposed ban on minarets in 2009. Voter participation was low at 56% but the result had to be accepted.

In contrast to the European Citizens' Initiative, which is an agenda-setting tool for deliberative democracy, Switzerland has a system of binding direct democracy. It is not as if the borders will suddenly become closed since the government has three years to implement the provision with legislation and negotiate with the EU. It is difficult to imagine however how a quota system, which has now become a democratically established right, can be reconciled with the European rights to free movement. This vote therefore could signal an end to the EU-Swiss agreement on the free movement of persons signed in Luxembourg on 21 June 1999, which was also approved in a referendum held less than three years ago.

This affects 1.15 million foreign workers in Switzerland or 23% of the Swiss workforce, but also a further 453,000 Swiss citizens living throughout the EU. Commentators have also pointed out that this referendum could be a counterproductive blow to the high performing Swiss economy and standard of living it was designed to protect. Moreover, the free movement agreement contains a "guillotine clause", which if broken, automatically triggers termination of six other bilateral agreements with the EU on transport, agriculture, technical standards, government procurement, scientific and technical co-operation. Politicians have reacted by pointing out that the agreement with the EU is not like a Swiss cheese, with holes in it, and that a pick and mix policy is not possible. The firm line taken by EU leaders may be influenced by the need to signal to the UK that an opt-out or renegotiation of free movement of people to and from the UK should not be possible whilst maintaining full participation in the other three "commercial" freedoms of the internal market.

Scaremongering about "benefit tourists"

A typical theme, often fuelled by eurosceptical or right wing political forces is that free movement paves the ways for so-called "benefit tourists." On 7 March 2013 four ministers of the interior for the UK, Germany, Austria and the Netherlands wrote to the EU Council President pointing out that some municipalities were being "put under considerable strain by certain immigrants from other member states (...) burdening the host countries' social welfare system".[68] They also drew attention to their need, whilst supporting free movement as a fundamental right, to defend the rights of their own citizens. There is however very little evidence of "benefit tourism", despite differences in levels of member states' welfare benefits, which in theory could be exploited by European citizens practising their rights to free movement within the EU.[69]

Despite this, restrictions on free movement became a major plank in the bid by the UK government to renegotiate their terms of membership of the EU, the results of which were put to the in-out referendum. In a speech on 26 November 2014, the Prime Minister, David Cameron did not go so far as to demand "emergency brakes" or quantitative restrictions on intra-EU migration. The five proposed measures would however have an equivalent effect, creating a new class of European citizens in waiting:

– To deport EU job-seekers who have not found work within six months; and to stop such job-seekers accessing 'universal credit' (which will incorporate the current job-seeker's allowance) when it is rolled out from 2015 onwards, for their first four years in Britain.
– To impose a four-year period before EU migrants have access to in-work benefits like tax credits and housing benefit.
– To stop workers in one EU Member State collecting child benefit there for children who live in another Member State.

---

68 Letter from Austria, Germany, Netherland and UK to Irish President Upson R. available at http://www.statewatch.org/news/2013/apr/eu-4-ms-welfare-letter-to-irish-presidency.pdf.
69 In "COM/2013/0837 final. Free movement of EU citizens: Five actions to make a difference" the Commission states, "recent studies conclude that there is no statistical relationship between the generosity of the welfare systems and the inflows of mobile EU citizens."

- To prevent workers from countries that join the EU from seeking work in the rest of the EU and these countries' economies have partially converged with those of the existing members.
- To make it easier to deport criminals, fraudsters and beggars from other Member States and to ban their re-entry.[70]

The threat to European rights to free movement is evident. It is also worrying that such speeches by leading politicians, which fail to make a clear distinction between free movement of people within the EU and immigration, will feed prejudice. The message and assumptions on which the speech is based are as negative as the proposals. For example: "And of course freedom of movement has evolved significantly over the years from applying to job-holders to job-seekers too; from job-seekers to their non-European family members; and from a right to work, to a right to claim a range of benefits."[71] This is a caricature of European citizenship.

In the outcome of the negotiations for a new relationship with the EU, the UK achieved results on all its demands, but less than the original objectives. The Member States in Central and Eastern Europe achieved some success in protecting the interests of their own nationals working in the UK. The European Council conclusions of 18-19 February 2016 were largely dismissed in the UK press as a weak compromise, which would have little effect on intra-EU migration. Instead of a blanket ban on access to in-work benefits for up to four years for newly arrived EU workers, the UK obtained an emergency brake which instead of being permanent is limited to 7 years, the equivalent timescale applied for transitional arrangements for new Member States. The arrangement resembles a retrospective compensation to the UK for not having applied the transitional arrangements on the occasion of the 2004 enlargement. To be able to apply the brake, assuming the referendum on 23 June 2016 had resulted in a vote to stay in the EU, the UK first had to show that its in-work benefits were a significant pull factor creating an artificial burden on public finances. The EU would then authorise limitations on access to benefits for up to 4 years, but on a graduated basis starting with complete exclusion, but gradually increasing access to benefits. Flying in the face of all its previous

---

70 Summary by the Centre for European Reform titled "Cameron's migration speech and EU law: Can he change the status quo", 4 December 2014. Available from: http://www.cer.org.uk/.

71 David Cameron's EU speech, 28 November 2014. Full text available on the BBC website: http://www.bbc.com/news/uk-politics-30250299.

statements and evidence collected about the benefits of freedom of movement of workers who pay more in taxes than they receive in benefits, the Commission claimed that the type of exceptional situation the proposed emergency brake is intended to cover existed. On what basis? Such measures discriminate directly against citizens of other Member States denied access to benefits given to domestic workers. Over time more progressive ideas to tackle the negative side effects of free movement of workers whilst keeping it free should prevail: the proposal made in this book for a free movement solidarity fund is the opposite of the emergency brake.

The settlement was the lesser of two evils but it was reached by governments for the first time showing a collective desire to control free movement and was by far the most difficult and controversial of the UK demands. The negative tone of the document is striking and sets a dangerous precedent for other governments to raise alleged difficulties caused by freedom of movement. The emergency brake has to be seen together with the other concessions won by the UK. It may seem reasonable that benefits paid to a worker's children left back home should be calculated according to the cost of living in that home state, but this penny pinching restriction could well encourage other attempts to limit benefits. The settlement with the UK also overturned the Metok judgement (Case C-127/08) described in chapter 2. It will now be required that third country nationals should have prior legal residence in another Member State before joining their EU family members in the host state. There was an attempt to broaden the scope for Member States to be able to expel EU citizens from their territory, since past and not only actual behaviour which could be a threat to public order can be taken into account. This collective governmental interference with European citizens' rights should not come as a surprise, but more as open confirmation of the more hidden barriers to freedom of movement described in chapter 5, in the areas where Member States are seeking to limit their social security payments or the family reunion of third country nationals.

With the majority vote to leave the EU, by 52% to 48% UK citizens lose their European citizenship and the Council settlement of February 2016 becomes irrelevant in theory. It could however be resurrected in case of a "soft" BREXIT meaning an association close to membership, rather than a "hard" BREXIT. In its paper on the process of withdrawing from the European Union (Cm 9216 of February 2016), the UK government explained that the only possible route for exit is through applying Article 50 of the Treaty on the European Union. This Article has not been used before and there will therefore be a longer and more serious period of uncertainty this time for both 1.5 million UK citizens living in the EU and 2.5 million EU citizens in the UK, this total of some 4 million representing nearly one third of those according to Eurostat permanently living and working in another Member State. The impact of BREXIT will be experienced throughout the EU. It is not surprising that increasing numbers of British citizens with a family connection to Ireland are considering dual citizenship, whilst EU citizens in the UK are wondering whether they should take on British citizenship since their European status will not count any more. A decision to opt now for dual citizenship rather than wait for the outcome of the UK's terms of settlement with the EU is understandable. The process described in Article 50 is weighted in favour of the existing 27 Member States, which first draw up guidelines among themselves before opening talks with the UK. The UK government paper draws attention not only to the uncertainties of the procedure, but also the breadth of the issues which have to be negotiated after 40 years of membership. How to ensure that European citizens' rights are given priority when there will be so much lobbying for economic interests? Article 50 provides that "The Treaties shall cease to apply to the State in question" (and therefore to European citizenship) "once a withdrawal agreement is reached or failing that for two years, unless there is a unanimous agreement to prolong that period for a further two years". The most likely scenario is that UK citizens will be "European citizens on the way out" for a four-year period. How long beyond that would it take for a settlement to be implemented? No one knows, but it is estimated that it would take the UK outside the EU up to 10 years to negotiate trade deals. Those directly impacted by BREXIT could face a longer period of uncertainty. This makes it very difficult to plan one's own and one's children's future.

During this period, there are likely to be increasing difficulties and tensions at certain borders: Calais, the border between Northern Ireland and the Republic, or Gibraltar. UK pensioners may well find their residence and access to health care and other public services becoming open to challenge in Spain and other Southern European countries. Rights to work and remain in the UK for many EU citizens, particularly from the new Member States in Central and Eastern Europe may well be called in question coupled with the EU demands to exert control over free movement of people from the UK. The longer the period of uncertainty lasts, the more likely it is that tensions will accumulate which will make the final settlement harder to achieve. For this settlement, there is a choice between the UK remaining part of the internal market and having to accept in return free movement of persons, or there could be a settlement of a different kind in which case there is no guarantee of European rights continuing in their present form. The calculation of pensions by totalling work periods in different EU Member States in case of BREXIT will be a major issue for UK citizens who have retired in the EU, those who have worked in the EU and retired in the UK and European citizens who have worked in the UK. The last page of the UK government document on the process for withdrawing from the European Union contains a commitment to uphold acquired rights.

The document states "there would be no requirement under EU law for these rights to be maintained if the UK left the EU". Should an agreement be reached to maintain these rights, the expectation must be that this would be reciprocated for EU citizens in the UK. The assumption made by the government is that such an agreement might be reached in the context of the UK joining the European Economic Area (EEA) with a similar status to that of Norway requiring that in exchange for access to the internal market, free movement of persons to and from the UK would be maintained. But this will never be easily accepted by many in the 'leave' campaign. The argument on the EU side and one which has been made for example following the referendum on 9 February 2014 in Switzerland in favour of immigration quotas, is that the four modern commercial freedoms of people, goods, services and capital are indissoluble. In turn, however, the UK Government will have a mandate to negotiate tougher restrictions and emergency brakes on EU citizens than those agreed in February. Even if in the most optimistic scenario the core of the European rights might well be preserved, although with additional restrictions, their enforcement will be an uphill struggle. This is especially so since EU governments and institutions consider that in the February 2016 agreement they gave the UK an opportunity to accept a generous concession which would have been rejected. There is no guarantee however that this will happen and that the UK will stay part of the internal market. In which case the rights or some of them listed in the government document will disappear and the rest of this description of a possible BREXIT scenario becomes irrelevant.

The main issue in the area of free movement of persons is the gap between the fine principles of European law and the way European rights face numerous obstacles and red tape on the ground. If the UK remains part of the internal market, its citizens will still be able to use EU assistance services for citizens and businesses such as Europe Direct, Your Europe Advice and Solvit. For more serious complaints it would be possible to go to a 'surveillance authority' or have the case referred from a national court to a special EFTA-EEA Court which exists alongside the CJEU in Luxembourg. However, whilst support outside the EU from the UK government would become more important, the latter would not be party to legislative decisions which affect internal market rules and European rights – it is a question of "co-shaping" not "co-deciding". A number of joint expert, ministerial and parliamentary committees bring together EU decision-makers and the representatives of neighbouring states which are part of the internal market, but these are not effective forums for raising and solving citizens' concerns. The government would be part of the internal market, subject to EU decisions but without participating in decision-making in the EU institutions. The position of UK citizens would mirror that of the government being part of the internal market but without the European arm of their citizenship. To an increasing extent, European rights in the internal market beyond the EU are shaped by the European court's case law based on the citizenship articles which can only be invoked by EU citizens, rather than EEA citizens.

There is no reason why people in the UK, like many in Switzerland or Norway, should not feel just as much European citizens as those in the EU, even without the formal status of EU citizen. The loss of Union citizenship which in terms of Article 20 TFEU is linked to one country being a member of the EU may not result in the loss of all the rights associated with that status, but it will make access to the appeal mechanisms which are responsible for their enforcement much more difficult. There is no reason why UK citizens should not petition the European Parliament, but the extent to which the Petitions Committee takes up a petition and hears its representatives depends on its substance and political importance. A petition from those who do not vote in European elections is inevitably a second order petition. Using other channels to appeal or defend European rights with the EU Institutions is even more difficult. The European Ombudsman deals with complaints from EU citizens or organisations with a registered office in Member States. Using the EU's freedom of information or access to documents regime is also subject to citizenship or residence in the EU. Only EU citizens over the age of 18 can sign a European Citizens' Initiative (ECI), whereby a minimum of 1 million people demand that the Commission presents a new law.

Anyone examining the annual reports relating to these mechanisms for access and appeal or looking through the register of ECIs will understand that they are in their infancy. As awareness of European rights increases and possibilities expand through social media for collecting signatures across national borders, the importance of channels of communication between citizens and the EU institutions will increase. The fact that they will be beyond the reach of British citizens is problematic not only for the defence of their European rights, but also when internal market rules more generally apply to the UK. BREXIT is also a setback for all reformers pushing for a more transparent, accountable and democratic EU – they will lose support from an important part of the EU's active citizens even if the departure of the UK government is no great loss.

Free movement of people, although apparently the EU's most popular achievement is being contested to an increasing extent. In this chapter, it is argued that whilst overall free movement is a win-win situation for countries of origin, host countries and European migrants themselves, there are inevitable failures and local problems because of its uneven spread. It is not though because of this, that calls for restrictions on European rights should be allowed to succeed. On the contrary, the emphasis should be on defending European rights by stepping up enforcement to make sure that they work better, whilst dealing locally with local problems. The European Union has emerged from an enlargement process where "transitional arrangements" and overall restrictions on free movement rights for European citizens from new Member States created more problems than they solved. There should now be emphasis on giving cities and local authorities more power and resources to manage effectively the impact of free movement of people, where there is a demonstrated impact in selective regions. Evidence suggests that although messages about the overall benefits of intra-EU migration and progress towards a European labour market should be part of the response to scaremongering about free movement, they are not enough. The message has to address local communities and the facts on the ground. This is why in chapter 5, a mixed approach is advocated: improving enforcement of European rights on the one hand, creating a European free movement solidarity fund on the other. Since free movement and mobility in all its forms within the EU are practiced by far more people than official statistics suggest, any further restrictions are likely to affect a disproportionally large number of people-and therefore must be resisted.

CHAPTER 4 What wide-open challenges for the future of European citizenship?

In the preceding chapters, we have shown that European citizenship has deeper historical roots, has been developed substantially by the Court of Justice of the European Union and is more widely practiced than generally recognised. Whilst in 2013, the European Union organised a special year to celebrate the 20th anniversary of the inclusion of Union citizenship in the Maastricht Treaty, it could have been the 60th anniversary. Why therefore has not more been done to develop Union citizenship? Why is there a "general failure to harness the resonance of citizenship as a political and legal concept?"[72] In this chapter, we consider the obstacles and a series of questions about the development of European citizenship. We need to explore further why European citizenship is both such a popular and contested concept.

(i) How to make European citizenship more popular?

Despite its solid legal foundations, European citizenship has failed to capture the popular imagination. And yet there is nothing to suggest on the basis of evidence from opinion polls that this should not be possible. Although the European Union and the benefits of membership have lost support, particularly since the onset of the economic crisis, the extent to which people see themselves as European citizens has held up remarkably well. The Standard Eurobarometer of autumn 2013 shows a general downward trend as far as the image of the EU is concerned. In the first half of 2005, 50 % of respondents still had a positive image of the EU; by autumn 2013, the figure had shrunk to 31%. On the other hand, the extent to which people see themselves as European citizens is on the increase. Does this amount to convincing support, or simply a recognition of being first and foremost a citizen of a country and secondly to some degree a European

---

72 Shaw, J. *Citizenship: Contrasting Dynamics at the Interface of Integration and Constitutionalism.* European University Institute (EUI), Working Paper RSCAS 2010/60. San Domenico Di Fiesole: EUI, 2010.

citizen? Of the 65% who feel that they are European citizens in some way, only a quarter claim that they are "definitely" European, whilst only 6% see themselves as more European than a citizen of their country.[73] If the majority in the middle see themselves as both a national and a European citizen, surely one can be optimistic about the first transnational citizenship of the modern era? This is especially the case since the percentages recognising that they are European citizens are much higher among young people.

The surveys do however suggest that the majority in favour of European citizenship is not much more than passive approval. First of all, the overall picture still shows that a generation after making Union citizenship a formal status, 34% of people on average still do not see themselves as European, only national citizens, an EU average which can rise to over half the population in more eurosceptical countries even two-thirds in the UK, where people do not see themselves as part of the European family. In political discourse, "EU citizens" refers to people from the 27 Member States living in the UK whereas those from the UK living abroad in the EU are referred to as British citizens. Neither the "Remain" nor the "Leave" campaign warned voters that in case of BREXIT they would lose their EU citizenship. The main obstacle to the development of European citizenship and the emergence one day of a European public sphere lies in the differences across countries in attitudes towards European integration and other factors, such as language skills. Within all countries there is a socio-economic rift, with a sense of European citizenship predominating among those with enough resources and well-educated enough to enjoy the opportunities this status offers, whereas those who do not have such advantages, simply do not relate to such a concept. This emerges clearly from all the Eurobarometer opinion polls: it is the greatest of the societal challenges to European citizenship, since above all else "citizenship is a condition of civic equality."[74] Such socio-economic and geographical rather than political divisions were apparent in the French and Dutch votes to reject the Constitutional Treaty in 2005 and in the UK vote to reject membership of the EU in 2016. These are not purely national phenomena and could well occur elsewhere.

---

73 Standard Eurobarometer no 81 spring 2014. It is possible using the search engine to track answers to the questions about being a European citizen over time.
74 Bellamy, R. *Citizenship: A Very Short Introduction.* Oxford, Oxford University Press, 2008.

It is difficult to avoid the impression that support for European citizenship remains at a superficial level and is perhaps more fragile than its proponents would like to imagine. This is born out by contrasting opinion polls. For example, whilst Eurobarometer polls suggest that 40% of people are aware of their European rights – a percentage that has increased, 56% of the population regard free movement of people as the most positive achievement of the EU (alongside the Euro and the preservation of peace) and an even larger majority – 67% - good for the economy in their own country.[75] National polls suggest the opposite with a majority considering that EU migrants should not be able to access social benefits before they have paid into the system for a number of years.[76] The answers depend very much on the questions put. As we have seen in the previous chapter, linking free movement of people to fear of migration with scaremongering about welfare tourism has an impact on public opinion, which may be volatile and open to persuasion.

What people think of something so complex as European citizenship cannot in any case be gathered from opinion polls alone, where there is always the temptation to give what one considers the politically correct answer. This is why, to engage with citizens one has to go back to the question of "what is European citizenship?" and to find out more, involve them in seeking answers, not just by random surveys, but also by participatory processes across European countries. Bringing together the scattered elements of European citizenship as proposed in the guidelines can contribute to raising awareness and stimulating debate. Despite all the opinion polls, extensive sociological surveys and European projects, there have never been participatory pan-European debates involving representative groups of the population of EU Member States about what it means to be a European citizen. This is why in chapter seven it is recommended that that is precisely what should be done.

---

75   Standard Eurobarometer no. 365 of February 2013.

76   For more information read "Social rights of EU migrant citizens: A comparative perspective", 2015 by BEUCITIZEN. Available from: http://beucitizen.eu/wp-content/uploads/Deliverable-6.1_final1.pdf.
See also Van Oorshot, W. "Making the difference in social Europe: deservingness perceptions among citizens of European welfare states", *Journal of European Social Policy*, Vol. 16, No. 1, pp. 23-42, 2006.

(ii) How to overcome the reluctance of governments to develop European citizenship?

As we have seen in the introduction, the Spanish initiative to include Union citizenship in the Treaty at Maastricht was seen as a first step to be followed by others. The attitude of governments has however been historically much more supportive of European citizenship as long as it remained an aspiration to build a peoples' Europe, to become much more cautious once it took on legal existence. In part this reflects the difficult climate in which the Maastricht Treaty was ratified by a slender majority in the referendum in France. The Treaty was then rejected in a first referendum in Denmark before assurances and opt-outs were sufficient to obtain a majority in a second referendum. The introduction of the right to vote and stand in local elections was also controversial, particularly in regions where numbers of European citizens are significant and where their votes could change the outcome. In chapter 2 we have described these difficulties and divergent opinions about the introduction of Union citizenship in the Maastricht Treaty.In the run up to the following Treaty reform at Amsterdam in 1997, there was expectation that Union citizenship would be further developed, but caution prevailed: any addition of new rights should be "appropriate" to citizenship as such, rather than universal, whilst "no direct effect should derive from the inclusion of new rights in the Treaty" and the costs of implementing them should be assessed.[77] No significant progress was made therefore, except a clarification, to reflect Danish concerns, that Union citizenship should be complementary and in no way replace national citizenship.

The next opportunity to develop Union citizenship through Treaty reform came with the 2001 Laeken declaration by which the Convention on the Future of Europe was set up.[78] Could it not be expected that Union citizenship would be developed in this context, since the objective was a

---

77 Council Presidency introductory note on citizenship of 26 July 1996 (Conf/ 3878/96). As a consequence a general anti-discrimination clause was added to the Treaty at Amsterdam which could not be invoked directly in a Court by European citizens. At the same time, the European Court was beginning to establish Union citizenship by linking it to equal treatment on the grounds of nationality as having direct effect. European Union law is more effective against some forms of discrimination than others, a point raised in the guidelines.

78 See "Laeken Declaration on the Future of the European Union, 15 December 2001".

constitutional settlement?[79] Amendments to the chapter on Union citizenship were rejected and the status quo maintained. Members explained that their overriding priority was to take over the work of a previous Convention and make the Charter of Fundamental Rights legally binding and part of the new Treaty. If they had attempted at the same time to strengthen Union citizenship, both objectives could have failed. On the other hand, the texts emerging from the Convention made citizenship part of the Treaty rhetoric giving citizens a more prominent status, no longer referring to peoples but to citizens of Europe. A link was made between European citizens and elections to the European Parliament. Aware perhaps that rhetoric and a general call to create a European public sphere was not enough, the Convention accepted a proposal to introduce citizens' initiatives, whereby one million European citizens could demand a European law. Rather than address the issue of citizenship as such, the Convention took the classic route of the European Union and introduced specific reforms.

The reforms introduced by the Convention were insufficient to convince voters since the Constitutional Treaty was decisively defeated in the referenda in France and the Netherlands in 2005 and quickly abandoned, even though paradoxically it contained reforms to bring the EU closer to citizens. The reaction of governments when the contents were taken over in the Treaty of Lisbon was to strip the text of constitutional elements, such as the primacy of EU law, the flag, and the anthem (Beethoven's ode to joy) and motto resulting from the "will of the citizens and States of Europe to build a common future." This makes little difference since the symbols are still used, but seen from the standpoint of developing a common citizenship, it is a setback. An additional practical symbol is proposed in the final chapter, where it is suggested that a European citizenship card should be introduced. The climate surrounding the negotiations leading to the Treaty of Lisbon was secretive, but it was apparent that the delegation of the European Parliament had to insist that Union citizenship still had a prominent mention in the Treaty on European Union ,which was indeed achieved (see Article 9 TEU),despite the reluctance of governments.

---

79 Jean-Luc Dehaene, Vice President of the Convention and responsible for relations with civil society explained that this position taken by several NGOs was based on a misunderstanding: the objective was not a constitution, but a Constitutional Treaty.

In none of the Treaty reforms following Maastricht was any proposal made by governments or EU Institutions to change the weak evolutionary clause, Article 25 TFEU, despite the progress made generally to strengthen the legislative powers of the European Parliament and introduce majority voting in the Council of Ministers. It should be recalled that in terms of Article 25, the Commission reports every three years on activities related to Union citizenship and may make proposals. But these are subject to assent rather than legislative amendment by the European Parliament and unanimity in the Council of Ministers. Through successive Treaty revisions post Maastricht, governments and EU Institutions have shown increasing reluctance to develop European citizenship as such. It may have reached a certain limit, which is an invitation for civil society to take up the challenge to fight for its further development, as argued in the last chapter.

(iii) National and European citizenship complement each other, but is the European dimension strong enough?

From the limited evidence of opinion polls (see (i) above), there appears to be a capacity on the part of most people to conceive citizenship at different levels and to accommodate quite naturally the idea of being primarily a citizen of a country and secondly a European citizen. Experience with advising people about overcoming barriers to free movement suggests that most see their European rights as a direct consequence of being a national of a Member State, rather than following from European citizenship as an independent source of law. The ease with which different levels of citizenship can be seen as complimentary, rather than in conflict with each other, is also suggested by new approaches to citizenship education which tend to embrace both national characteristics and more universal values and human rights. Education for national citizenship far from undermining or being in competition with education for European citizenship can support it. In part II, the final chapter points to the spread of citizenship education across Europe since the fall of the Berlin wall, from which European citizenship could benefit if there was a clearer idea of what it is and what to teach. Many can share the view that their identity is both rooted but can shift or even change.

There is still scope though for confusion between the practices of citizenship at different levels. When seen through the perspective of national citizenship with its constitutional guarantees, range of entitlements and financial solidarity mechanisms for free education, health, social welfare, and other public services, European citizenship can appear a poor relation, hardly worthy of its name. An early amendment to the Maastricht citizenship chapter in the Convention on the Future of Europe would have introduced "dual citizenship" both national and European. This overlooks the fact that the two citizenships are not comparable and the proposal was rightly rejected as confusing. European citizenship as shown for example in the case-law of the Court of Justice of the European Union is transnational – limited to what is necessary for the opening up in a non-discriminatory way of our respective citizenships to each other. This does not mean full-scale citizenship entitlements so much as the minimum necessary for their coordination and mutual recognition. To a limited extent also European citizenship is the means by which people can participate in European affairs, but falling far short of the rights and duties expected of citizens in a state (for example military service or jury duty). The danger of claiming too much for European citizenship, instead of situating it in its own transnational context distinct from national citizenship, is that there can be confusion between the two and rejection. In points 1-7 of the guidelines attached, a first attempt is made to highlight those rights and duties which are particularly necessary for a transnational citizenship to have meaning, rather than all those linked to the organisation of the citizenship of a state in a particular territory. It is much more a question of linking different citizenships, making life easier particularly for citizens from minority groups, mixed nationality, and a high level of mobility than creating a full-scale citizenship in its own right.

European citizens' rights depend for their delivery on the administrations of the Member States represented in the town halls, social security offices, and different ministries. Sorting out questions of access to social security entitlements and recognition of qualifications also depends on papers and certificates delivered by the country of origin. The links to national citizenship are always the overriding factor and key to overcoming barriers to living and working in another Member State without discrimination. The European dimension is all present but in no way operates independently of the national status brought across the border or of acceptance of this status in the country of destination. Thus there is no European social security system which would be necessary if there was a genuine European labour market, but coordination of national systems sufficient to allow for more limited freedom of movement. Moreover, although different national rates of income tax can influence where people live, establishing the rates is the exclusive competence of Member States. In normal circumstances freedom of movement is a discreet and controlled freedom, subject in practice to conditions, except if it is very short term and temporary since for stays of less than three months no formalities are necessary in the host country. If the Member States' administrations fail to agree which is responsible for example for the delivery of social security benefits to a European citizen living in one country but working in another, he or she can assert European rights as an independent source of law. This has been made clear in chapter 2 on the role of the Court of Justice of the European Union , but such cases are the exception rather than the rule. Most people are very reluctant to assert a European citizenship status against a national administration and would prefer quick practical compromises to lengthy and expensive litigation. The average person lacks the knowledge, time and money to embark on such a course even when it would be in their interests and help advance the cause of European citizenship.

What is true of free movement and European rights is also true of the relationship between the EU and the citizen more generally across the range of its other policies and symbols: "Yet the EU is not simply a supersized nation state. Instead, the EU's cultural infrastructure is rooted in a specific type of banal authority, which navigates national loyalties while portraying the EU as complementary to, not in competition with, local identities". [80] National and European identities are reverse sides of the same coin, quite literally so in the case of the euro coins. Similarly the standardised burgundy coloured passport is both national and European. The European and the national flags fly together, whilst the country holding the six month Presidency of the Council of Ministers is expected to promote itself as a tourist and business destination as much as it promotes Europe, not unlike the country which is host to the Eurovision song contest, albeit more discreetly. EU Institutions are not centralised in one "federal" location, but scattered whilst the EU specialised agencies are shared out right across all Member States. Deference is shown towards national interests, almost to the extent that they become indistinguishable from European interests. The question of which Member State should be host to

---

80 McNamara, K. *The Politics of everyday Europe: Constructing Authority in the European Union.* Oxford: Oxford University Press, p. 3, 2015.

a new European agency always leads to protracted negotiations in the Council of Ministers. If an attempt is made to emphasize the European at the expense of the national, a backlash can be expected. Thus, the negotiators of the Lisbon Treaty deliberately stripped the failed constitutional Treaty of its attempt to elevate the status of the European flag and anthem. More and more Euro coins and notes are circulating in the Euro-zone, thus Europeanising everyday life for some Europeans, but without imposing a strong European message.[81] The paper Euro currency is deliberately nondescript and not tied to a particular place, evoking through abstracted bridges and windows an image of some distant European cultural heritage. Equally significant is the way we are exposed to the evidence of European standardisation on the labels of everyday purchases or see the same signs for EU citizen queues at airports and a charter of our rights as European travellers. The question arises of whether the discreet reminders of the European dimension of citizenship which appear well designed for periods of relative harmony and economic growth are strong enough to withstand crises. As Kathleen McNamara points out in the preface to her book about the symbols of Europe complementary to national identity: "This deracination and localisation does produce a certain type of authority for the EU, but it is a strikingly banal authority compared to those political forms which went before. And it is therefore not well fashioned to stand up to the anti-EU populism that is sweeping Europe..."[82] European citizenship, like any citizenship, needs much more affirmative symbols.

(iv) How well does European citizenship fit with the decision-making processes of the European Union?

When Europe is discussed with the public, many people express doubt as to whether their voice can really count at EU level and others doubt whether this is even a course of action to be considered. For many there can be no true citizenship without statehood, so that the very concept of a European citizenship finding expression in the European Union appears irrelevant. Can one construct a European citizenship? Should there not be first a European constitution? The case for a European citizenship ex-

---

81 See Moro, G. (ed.) *The Single Currency and European Citizenship: Unveiling the Other Side of the Coin.* New York: Bloomsbury, 2013.

82 Ibid. 80.

pressed in terms of the opening up of our respective national territories to fellow Europeans is much clearer than enacting European citizenship towards the European Institutions. It is highly problematic to transpose to the level of the European Union the theories about the relationship between citizenship and the state. The EU structure is unique, combining structures which are intergovernmental with those that are more federal. The European Union has many of the features associated with the exercise of power: an independent European central bank, an executive, a directly elected Parliament and an independent court. There are also mechanisms for citizen participation added to the institutional mechanism: rules on access to documents, complaints procedures, petitions and a European ombudsman. There are a number of European agencies which have their national equivalents for data protection, food, or the environment.

In its institutional design the European Union does offer to a greater extent than any other international or European organisation opportunities for citizen involvement. This is particularly true of the normal legislative decision-making process. The tension between national and European interests is played out over successive stages, from which it is possible to assess when to act – hopefully collectively – at the national level or the European level to make one's voice heard. It is not the aim here to analyse the decision-making process in depth, but merely to refute the argument that citizens have no voice in European affairs.[83] At the start of the decision-making process, there is a public consultation process and in some but not all of the 28 Member States, consultations at national level. The proposal then goes from the Commission to the European Parliament, and consultative bodies. The European Economic and Social Committee (EESC) and the Committee on the Regions (CoR) are useful access points for citizens. Members of the European Parliament (MEPs) often declare that they would like to hear more from citizens, not just organised lobbies. The extent to which MEPs communicate with citizens, are present on social media or in their local offices, and are open to receive complaints depends, to a large extent, on their own efforts and priorities. Could there be a more systematic link between MEPs and citizens is an issue between elections and not just one for reform of the way the European Parliament is elected every five years. For example the national offices which the

---

83 For a fuller analysis of how citizens can voice concern with the EU see "12 tips for the Would-be European lobbyist " available at http://ecas.org/12-tips-european-lobbyist/.

European Parliament shares with the Commission in the capitals could be upgraded to become part of an EU-28 public sphere. The relative openness of the EU Institutions by comparison with their national counterparts does make them a privileged terrain for citizen action through consumer, environmental, public health or human rights groups, whether on issues of climate change, tobacco control, or the EU's foreign policy stance. At the same time, whilst there are undoubtedly success stories, obstacles to citizen involvement to influence distant decision-making processes need to be identified in order to see where reforms are necessary. In addition to practical considerations of time and cost, citizens also face a number of challenges which are more institutional in putting forward claims to the EU, and to which we now turn: issues of legal competence, complexity and secrecy in areas of decision-making and top-down crisis management

The issues around EU legal competence

As already pointed out there is a tendency to view citizenship through the lens of being a national of a Member State with the full range of rights, entitlements and responsibilities that it implies. In Articles 3-6 of the Treaty on the functioning of the European Union (TEFU), the division of competences between the EU and Member States does make it clear that what can be done at European level is far less than at national level. Exclusive EU competencies are limited to areas such as trade policy and competition. Competencies shared with national governments relate to the internal market and a range of other policies such as environment and consumer protection. Supporting competencies, where the EU can only intervene to support or coordinate, exclude legislative measures and connect precisely to those areas which go to the heart of what it means to be a citizen: education, public health, or culture. On the website for European citizens' initiatives, there is a warning about the issue of competence. Nevertheless, nearly half of the initiatives proposed have not even been able to collect one signature, since their registration has been refused by the Commission on the grounds that they have no legal basis in the Treaty.[84] There

---

84 For a full picture of the record with ECIs over the last 3 years go to: http://ec.europa.eu/citizens-initiative/public/welcome. On this website the Commission publishes the letters giving reasons for the rejection of ECIs. See also chapter 7 on ECI's.

is a clear tendency for citizens when raising issues with the European Union to be pushing at the boundaries of EU competence. Even the European citizens' initiatives (ECIs), accepted were calling for more value-based legislation, invoking the Charter of Fundamental Rights. Thus for example, one of the four ECIs which collected over 1 million signatures claimed that water should be treated as a human right not as a commodity. The ECI on media pluralism was as much concerned with freedom of expression and issues of government interference with the media, which is on the margin of EU competence, as with the issues of competition and of concentration of ownership, which are core concerns. In part II we will return to this issue and proposals to make citizens' initiatives more workable. Clearly the European citizen has to be more than just a good European: he or she has to be knowledgeable about the scope and limits of EU competence.

The complexity of EU affairs and the professional lobbying environment

In theory the decision-making process is open to input by citizens and civil society organisations, but in practice reforms are necessary and not just limited to ECIs. Whilst the Institutions, and in particular the Council of Ministers, have become much more open, there are still areas where decisions are taken behind closed doors: for example negotiations between the Commission, the European Parliament and Council on legislation or trade negotiations, even where these like the transatlantic trade and investment partnership (TTIP) have an impact on domestic standards. To mention another example: the negotiations with the UK in the European Council about the terms of that country's membership of the EU, the results of which were put to a referendum on 23rd June 2016, were held in total secrecy.

Further transparency in the Institutions is clearly insufficient if citizens remain aware that there is a vast lobbying constituency round the EU but do not see its precise legislative footprint and which organisations are lobbying on which issues with what resources. Whilst making the transparency register more complete, up-to-date and mandatory may help, it is only a step towards encouraging citizens to have their say. In theory this is provided by public consultations but these have become part of the increasingly technical and professionalised gathering of expertise round the Commission, rather than an instrument of participatory democracy. "Public" consultations can become more genuinely accessible to the public, but it is argued in chapter 7 that there should be a special law too in order make citizen deliberations a new pillar of EU decision-making.

Crisis management in the European Council

Whilst the normal decision-making processes or "community method" and appeal mechanisms of the EU do give citizens a tenuous foothold, the same is not true of intergovernmental decision-making outside this framework, and in particular during the last eight years of Euro-zone crisis management. The core of the process has been multiple sessions of the heads of government meeting in the European Council. This body has a permanent secretariat and President, but no law-making capacity. Crisis management has taken the form of, on the one hand, driving the community method and borrowing its institutions from the top down, and on the other, elaborating new intergovernmental Treaties. This may explain the paradox of a period of intense debate fuelled by media reports of the crisis meetings accompanied by very low levels of public engagement in European public consultations, for example. Legal commitments and conditions for loans or bailouts to the notoriously called PIGS (Portugal, Ireland, Greece and Spain) have been administered by the unelected TROIKA of the European Central Bank, the European Commission and the International Monetary Fund. It is not surprising that citizens hit by unemployment and cuts in public expenditure – even in the case of Greece with the overnight closing of public service television – took to the streets rather than believing that acting as European citizens towards the European Institutions would have any effect.

Collective decision-making treating the European economy as a whole gives way to disciplines on each national government having a deep effect on their prerogatives to set levels of public expenditure and organise health and education policies, for example, areas normally outside EU competence. Ironically, a category of ECIs were rejected on legal grounds even though they related to demands to protect social welfare systems, the most vulnerable in society and low wage earners from austerity measures decided by the European Union itself.[85] Crisis management has made the division of competences between national and European decision-making less clear thus adding to the sense of powerlessness for citizens. It is not enough to claim that the governments have a mandate from their electorate, particularly when representing them at the highest political level. Such a system resembles that of a constitutional monarchy or Kafka's Castle. Jürgen Habermas rightly points to the problem of the governments negotiating outside their territory with their voters left behind especially when those decisions impact clearly on domestic policies and budgets. "A transfer of sovereign rights does not diminish the scope of civic autonomy only on the condition that the citizens of the one affected state co-operate with the citizens of the other affected states in making supranational law in accordance with a democratic procedure."[86] The European citizens' initiatives attempted to meet this condition in response to the crisis and austerity measures, but failed.

The European decision-making processes are a significant challenge to effective citizen involvement. The reforms introduced by the Lisbon Treaty for example create new possibilities both to defend European rights more effectively and propose new rights with the legally binding Charter of Fundamental Rights and citizens' initiatives. But the Lisbon Treaty also further institutionalised the role of the European Council and intergovernmental decision-making remote from the normal legislative process in which citizens have at least some say. When to act and where - as a national or a European citizen - is often more complex in practice than the textbook description of the decision-making processes and the division of competences between the EU and the Member States. Reforms and additional instruments for participation are necessary before anyone can state positively that European citizenship fits the decision-making processes of the European Union. This is particularly the case with a Treaty which in some ways brings the citizens closer to the EU, but in others widens the gap.

---

85 This paradox was pointed out by the European Ombudsman in a speech to ECI Day 2016 at the EESC, available at http://www.ombudsman.europa.eu/activities/speech.faces/en/66538/html.bookmark.

86 Habermas, J. *The Crisis of the European Union: A Response*. Cambridge: Policy Press Cambridge, 2012.

(v) If EU citizenship is the basic foundation, could a European citizenship be conceived beyond it, based on shared values?

Whilst there is a need to strengthen the ways citizens can become involved with the European Union, it is difficult to avoid the conclusion that European citizenship must represent in peoples' minds something broader on a continental scale, even though Europe is a continent without clear fixed boundaries. If European citizenship is conceived only in the formal legal terms of the Maastricht Treaty, linked to nationality of an EU Member State, where does this leave for example the inhabitants of Iceland, Liechtenstein, Norway or Switzerland? Where does it leave the citizens of the UK or another Member State deciding to withdraw from the EU? They could consider themselves just as much European citizens as the majority within the EU, and in practice may well enjoy the same European rights to free movement. There are also those citizens from countries in the Western Balkans or Turkey who have applied for membership of the EU, who are European citizens in waiting. Then there are those in the Ukraine who have demonstrated in 2013 in Kiev for a European dream which appears to be fading within the EU. There were those demonstrating at the same time in Taksim Square in Istanbul who wanted to see their country more linked to Europe. Could a wider European citizenship emerge? After all, many of the EU programmes such as for those for life-long learning or research stretch beyond the EU borders as does support for civil society.

Such a challenge is worth taking up for a citizenship conceived on a continental scale has both more resonance and is a step towards the dream of cosmopolitan citizenship. This would be a signal that the European Union is not a finished structure, but open to other European states which share its values. It would also be a reminder of the broader European dimension when the European Union is being pushed because of the difficulties of reaching agreement among 28 Member States to considering increasing recourse to regional groupings or an advance guard able and willing to go faster than the rest, particularly in the Eurozone. [87] The message should be that there is no two–speed Europe for citizens, who are equal regardless of whether or not they come from the states which have adopted the Euro or are in the Schengen. Admittedly such a broad European cit-

---

87 For an authoritative argument in favour of a two-speed Europe see Piris, J. *The Future of Europe: Towards a Two-Speed EU?* Cambridge: Cambridge University Press, 2011.

izenship would be far from perfect with some citizens more equal than others, but it might one day be recognised that what we hold in common as Europeans is more important than such differences. For these reasons, the guidelines are a plea for a wider, outward-looking European citizenship.

It follows that a citizenship not related to a single institution or a fixed territory has to have some basis in a set of shared values. Reference is often made to "European values", particularly in opposition to violations of human rights. What these values are is nowhere explained in detail. When asked the question in opinion polls, European citizens describe European values in general terms of preserving peace, democracy and the rule of law which do not go far enough to answer the question of what we hold in common across Europe. Probably the best definition of European values is the Charter of Fundamental Rights, closely related to the Council of Europe convention on human rights of which it is a more modern version. To an increasing extent European values or finding "a new narrative for Europe"[88] is being invoked. However, as a group set up precisely to answer this question concluded: "a mere list of common European values is not enough to serve as the basis of European unity...This is because every attempt to codify "European values" is inevitably confronted by a variety of diverting national, regional, ethnic, sectarian and social undertakings."[89] To an increasing extent however citizenship is not so much about identity as linking different identities and values together. For that the Charter of Fundamental Rights to which we now turn provides the right broader context within which to situate European citizenship, bring its scattered elements together and so establish a basic consensus on which the sense of shared values can one day emerge more forcibly to help unite Europe in the face of crises.

---

88 This was the name given to a group of intellectuals assembled by the European Commission in 2013-2014.

89 European Commission, Institute for Human Science, Biedenkopf, K., Geremek, B., Michalski, K. *The Spiritual and Cultural Dimension of Europe* [online], Vienna/Brussels, October 2004.

PART TWO:
FINDING CINDERELLA

CHAPTER 5 Mind the gaps - how can European citizens' rights be better enforced and enlarged?

In theory, if citizenship is the "right to have rights", the EU is setting up a comprehensive structure. This is particularly so since the entry into force of the Lisbon Treaty which gives the Charter of Fundamental Rights the same value as the Treaties (Article 6 TEU) and requires the Union to become a party to the European Convention on Human Rights (ECHR). This may give individuals an ultimate right of appeal to the European Court of Human Rights in Strasbourg.[90] It places European citizens' rights in the broader framework of universal basic human rights and their more modern expression – for example condemning trafficking in persons as a form of slavery. The Charter makes "citizenship" one of six chapters, the others being dignity, freedom, equality, solidarity and justice. It places more emphasis on economic and social rights than the ECHR. According to one observer: "Citizenship of the European Union has finally acquired its Bill of Rights in the form of a legally binding EU Charter of Fundamental Rights; the skeleton that citizenship of the Union once was is now acquiring the flesh and blood it needs to merit the title."[91] This should involve however closing gaps in the structure: between the fine principles of European law and what happens in practice when people move round Europe, but also gaps in political rights and between European citizens and third country nationals.

In a similar way to Union citizenship itself, the impact of the Charter may be both less than hoped for by some, but more than just a codification of existing rights as claimed by others. Many citizens have been misled into believing that this is a general charter on human rights, whereas it is only applicable in areas where the EU has legal competence (Article 51). The Charter is an additional source of law citizens and their representa-

---

90 After years of hesitation in the context of Treaty revisions with Member States equally divided as to whether the Union should have its own separate charter or join the ECHR, the issues has been settled in favour of both steps.
91 Guild, E. *The European Union after the Treaty of Lisbon: Fundamental Rights and the EU citizenship.* EPS 'Liberty and Security in Europe/June 2010, Global Jean Monnet/European Community Studies Association, 2010.

tives can claim, particularly with the new rights to good administration (Article 41) and access to justice (Article 47). Those putting forward citizens' initiatives have found out that whilst quoting articles in the Charter may support their case, the only legal basis for legislative proposal lies in the Treaties. Given the development of case law (cf. Zambrano) attempts may be made to challenge internal violations of fundamental rights as have occurred recently in Bulgaria, Hungary, Poland or Romania, or systematic discrimination against minorities such as the Roma, as an infringement of the substance of Union citizenship. For example, the European Commission has accepted a citizens' initiative demanding that the EU takes a tougher stance to defend democracy and the rule of law in Hungary.[92]

The scope and limits of the Charter remain however to be defined. Any proposed legislation by the European Union has to be assessed in relation to the Charter, which is a first step towards more systematic application. This does not however address breaches of fundamental rights or challenges to the rule of law by Member States. There is a paradox: the EU has more power to enforce respect for the rule of law, fundamental rights and democratic values before a state has joined the EU as one of the criteria to become a member than it does after accession. This was shown to be the case when the Commission mounted technical challenges to Hungarian legislation infringing European law but without any clear impact on the policies of the government of Viktor Orbán. A step forward was however taken in March 2014 when the Commission presented a more comprehensive approach: a framework to safeguard the rule of law in the European Union.[93] This provided the basis for the European Commission to open an investigation of the rule of law in Poland in January 2016 after the new government passed legislation to bring the appointments to the Constitutional Tribunal under political control as well as undermine the independence of the media.[94] This will be a first test for a procedure whereby the

---

92 This initiative is called "Wake up Europe! Taking action to safeguard the European project", http://ec.europa.eu/citizens-initiative/public/initiatives/ongoing/details/2015/000005.

93 Speech by Viviane Reding titled "A new EU framework to safeguard the rule of law in the European Union" delivered on 18 March 2014.

94 BBC News, "EU launches probe into new Polish laws", 13 January 2016. Available from: http://www.bbc.com/news/world-europe-35303912. Lowe, J. "EU to investigate right-wing Polish government policies", *Newsweek,* 13 January 2016.

Commission investigates, discusses its findings with the Member State and makes recommendations. Even this non-judicial procedure provokes nationalistic and anti-EU attacks and could benefit from the support of a stronger sense of European citizenship. It is a procedure which can precede a possible application of Article 7 (TEU), described in political discourse as the "nuclear option", a measure of last resort. This is because the article contains a serious threat rather than lesser measures: "the Council, acting by a majority of four fifths of its members and after obtaining the assent of the European Parliament, may determine that there is a clear risk of a serious breach by a Member State of the values referred to in Article 2", the mission statement of the EU. It is not easy for the Council to reach such a conclusion, but when it does the result could be suspension of EU funds or voting rights.[95]

(i) Towards better enforcement of European rights

As citizens move in and out of different national systems more frequently, they become more knowledgeable about their rights, often quoting legislation and case law and therefore perceiving the gap between theory and practice. This makes it all the more necessary to close this gap by better enforcement. In a more nationalistic climate, with concerns over migration and cuts in social welfare budgets, Member States' administrations appear less cooperative. Enforcement is an uphill struggle. The Commission's role as an initiator of legislation tends to take precedence over that of "guardian of the Treaties" to ensure it is put into effect.

As we have seen, European citizenship is not detached from national citizenship, and does not have an existence in its own right, but is nevertheless distinct and transnational. The inevitable consequence of this ambiguity is that there are tensions between European rights to free movement and national rules and policies. In its case-law, the European Court attempts to strike a balance by declaring Union citizenship "a fundamental status" so that the citizen can invoke European free movement rights, which do not need to be justified. On the contrary the burden of proof is

---

Available from: http://europe.newsweek.com/democracy-courts-media-415146?rm=eu.

95 For the whole text of Article 7 (TEU) go to: http://eur-lex.europa.eu/legal-content/EN/TXT/?uri=celex%3A12012M007.

on national authorities to show that any restrictions of these rights are proportional and in the public interest. In practice, however, the cases which are resolved with an intervention by the courts or EU Institutions represent the tip of the iceberg. For people in work with recognised qualifications and an uncomplicated family life, European free movement can function, moreover, without apparent tensions. For job-seekers or less well-off citizens, the gap between the fine principles of European law and the way it is applied on the ground is more apparent. The burden of proof is shifted to the applicant with the administration seeking to apply the exception in the letter of the European rights, rather than their spirit. For many people on low incomes, those belonging to minorities or likely to suffer discrimination, the gap can be so significant that they question whether European citizenship has any meaning. Correct enforcement of the European Treaties and legislation, which is a priority for the European Commission, is essential to maintain a balance between European rights and national prerogatives. That is why emphasis is placed here on ways to strengthen enforcement and for citizens to play a more active role in defence of their European rights. Citizens should be involved in the attempts by the Commission and the Member States to resolve the tensions between European rights and national prerogatives. Without proper enforcement, European citizenship ceases to hold its own and becomes invisible beneath the weight of administrative practices connected to the national citizenships it is designed to link together. This is even more evident in a period of crisis and high unemployment.

There are three main areas where tensions become apparent in different ways between European rights and national prerogatives as a result in cuts in welfare budgets, concerns over immigration and differences in European values.

Social security and social benefits

Particularly since the onset of the financial and economic crisis, the public administration is under pressure to question claimants and in general has better access to personal data to be able to do so. In particular European citizens in a precarious situation, job seekers, and those on a low wage are facing increasing obstacles to obtain access to social security benefits, let alone social assistance. Too many vulnerable European citizens lose social rights in their country of origin before they access them in their new country of residence, falling into a limbo without protection. For those out of work, the requirement to have sufficient resources in order not to be a burden on the host Member State after three months in the country can become a reason for refusing a right of residence. Expulsions of European citizens for economic reasons have become more frequent increasing from zero in 2008 to over 2,700 in 2013 in Belgium for example.[96]

Family reunion and immigration

The single category most likely to be the victim of the tension between European rights and national policy is made up of family members, spouses or partners of a European citizen from a country outside the EU. The right of European citizens to move with their family member is held in tension with policies to combat illegal immigration. It is a kind of tension, which could only be reduced once Member States trust each others' policies on legal immigration and asylum and work towards a genuine common policy on immigration. As shown in chapter 2 on the Court of Justice of the European Union, the rights of mixed families of EU nationals and third country nationals can be upheld (see the Metock Case, C-127/08). However, applying EU law can result in decisions more favourable to immigrants than would have been possible under national law. In this way, free movement becomes associated with the failure of migration policy to control the numbers of immigrants.

The differences in family law and civil status

The decisions by the Court of Justice in relation to the acquisition and loss of citizenship, or how to reconcile different national laws and customs as to how one can name one's children all provide guidance as to the relationship between European and national citizenship. The same tensions

---

96 For an in-depth analysis on this issue see Maslowski, S. *The Expulsion of European Union Citizens from the Host Member State: Legal Grounds and Practice* available online on the Central and Eastern European Migration Review (CEEM) website: http://www.ceemr.uw.edu.pl/ and Lafleur, JM. *Restrictions in Access to Social Protection of New EU migrants to Belgium,* available at: http://www.eesc.europa.eu/resources/docs/33--jean--michel-lafleur.pdf.

arise when same-sex couples are discriminated against in Member States which do not recognise their civil partnership or marital status. There is even a failure by Member States to recognise the legal effects of civil partnerships such as joint ownership of property or inheritance rights. In the absence of EU legislation, Member States have exclusive competence, whilst being required by the case law of the European Court to take into account European rights to free movement.

The priority is to strengthen enforcement of European rights and the Commission's powers as guardian of the Treaties. As already stressed, far more attention has to be devoted to the uneven distribution of free movement and local action. In areas where free movement is heavily concentrated there should be use of EU cohesion policy and a special European free movement solidarity fund set up.[97] The tensions between European rights and national policies cannot be resolved only by enforcement of European rights and judicial means. Non-judicial, more decentralised local cross-border cooperation is also needed.

A change of culture is required, not only in the Commission, but also to commit the other Institutions and the Member States to give more priority to enforcement.[98]In another report, "Mind the gap – towards a better enforcement of European citizens' rights to free movement" this point is stressed as well whilst recommending a policy towards enforcement, which can be summarised as follows:

– *More emphasis on prevention is better than cure.* Legislation covering free movement of people takes the form generally of directives which establish common principles and objectives but leave it to each Member State to implement them according to their own legal and administrative practice. Although the so-called "citizenship directive" on free

---

97 This implies a more territorially based approach to European citizenship. In "La Citoyenneté européenne, un état quasi-étatique", published by Sciences Po, Paris in 2014, Teressa Pullano argues this point, rejecting the idea that citizenship of the Union is in some way a post-national phenomenon detached from the Member States territories.

98 This point is underlined by Alain Lamassure, member of the Eurpean Parliament in a report to the President of the French Republic: 'The citizen and the application of community law' 8 June 2008. Available from: http://www.alainlamassure.eu/ l.../975.pdf.
'Mind the Gap' was a report of a high level panel chaired by Sir David Edward, former judge of the European Court of Justice and drafted with the assistance of ECAS and Freshfields, Bruckhaus, Deringer (January 2010).

movement of European citizens does no more than reflect the case-law of the European Court, the Commission found that no single article had been correctly reflected in national law by all Member States.[99] In retrospect a binding requirement on Member States to notify in advance to the Commission any draft implementing measures, but also any other legislative measures, which could have affected implementation might have prevented the subsequent infringement procedures. Alternatively, such legislation could be recast as a regulation, which has the advantage of being directly applicable, without relying on correct enforcement through national implementing measures. In the current climate, however, new legislation is likely to be less protective of European citizens' rights.

- *A one-stop shop in each Member State to solve problems quickly.* As we have seen this takes the form at European level, of "Europe-Direct" with a free phone system which sends more difficult questions to Your Europe Advice or if more than just guidance is needed to SOLVIT, which aims to solve problems within 10 weeks. This deadline to instil a more problem-solving approach in the European administration should apply to all EU citizen assistance services, and in turn these should operate according to the same standards with a one-stop shop in each Member State. In the attached guidelines this is recommended in points 9 and 13.

- *Collective action by citizens.* The Commission has considerable discretion as to whether or not to act on individual complaints. An individual complaint may be an isolated instance of maladministration. To demonstrate that there is an infringement of EU law the Commission expects evidence from a number of complaints to indicate that there is a standard illegal practice. This is reasonable provided the Commission facilitates collective claims. Citizens have an interest in grouping their concerns and evidence together to give them greater weight with the Commission backing them up with a petition to the European Parliament or an appeal to a national court. When the Commission tries to persuade Member States to lift barriers to free movement rights, citi-

---

99 Report from the Commission on the application of Directive 2004/38 on the right of citizens of the Union and their family members to move and reside freely within the territory of the Member States (COM (2008) 840 final 10.12.2008. This conclusion was supported also in a study by ECAS for the legal affairs committee of the European Parliament (Pe 410/650).

zens need to make their presence felt as an unofficial third party. This is one reason why European citizenship needs its own civil society movement, as discussed in the final chapter.

- *A fast-track enforcement procedure.* It is relatively easy to send a complaint, but unless there is an immediate solution, it can take at least two years before the Commission appeals to the European Court of Justice and a further 18 months at least for judicial procedures. In the meantime the Member State(s) concerned can maintain the barrier to the exercise of European rights. The Commission should apply to the European Court to demand a Member State lift immediately any barrier to the exercise of European rights which prima farcie violates European law and affects a large number of people, pending full examination (an application for interim measures in terms of Article 279 TFEU).

- *A free movement solidarity fund.* In addition to making more effective use of European law to improve enforcement, action at the local level could also reduce tensions between European citizens on the move and the host country society. These tensions fuel demands for general restrictions on European rights and scaremongering about benefit tourists. However because free movement is so unevenly spread the real issues are exceptional instances of brain drain in countries of origin or strains on local services in host countries. EU cohesion policy, which brings together the European social and regional development and other funds, provides the right context for addressing these issues, combining a European framework with strong emphasis on local community development and partnership with all actors. A European free movement solidarity fund should be set up, not as a new instrument, but as part of the EU's cohesion policy. The fund should serve a dual purpose of supporting emergency help to vulnerable EU citizens, mentoring, language teaching and guidance for job seekers, whilst providing additional resources for local health, educational and housing services. The first objective would fall under the social fund, the second under its equivalent for regional development. There should be equal contributions to such a fund from the country of origin, the host country and the EU budget. There would be no reason in the operation of such a fund to attempt to make an artificial distinction between EU citizens and third country national migrants. Civil society organisations in countries of origin and countries of destination should have access to this fund to carry out joint projects supporting EU citizens before departure (80% of subsequent problems could be solved by better preparation and mentoring before departure) and then assisting with their integration in the host country and possibly return home. Much of the pattern of EU free movement is short-term and circular. The fund would support both local and cross-border operations giving substance to European citizenship in action.

(ii) *Allowing all citizens resident in other Member States to vote in national elections*

Whilst proper enforcement of existing rights is the priority for European citizens to demonstrate the practical added value of European citizenship, there are gaps in the rights. It is illogical that European citizens should be able to vote and stand in local and European elections in their country of residence, but not in the elections that really count – the national ones. It is against the spirit of EU law and the Council of Europe Convention on Human Rights that some European citizens taking advantage of free movement and residence rights, should be denied the possibility of voting and standing in national elections, either in their country of origin or the host country.[100] This is a stain on European democracy to which attention was drawn for example by a European citizens' initiative (ECI) "Let-me-vote"[101] which although far from succeeding in its objective of obtaining 1 million signatures, at least raised the issue. Being denied the main right to participate politically may explain why European citizens have been reluctant to make use of their existing rights in second-order elections.[102] Disenfranchisement in national elections in the country of residence is a powerful reminder to the European citizen that he or she is still a foreigner, since political rights are those most defining of citizenship. In a debate among the promoters of the "let-me-vote" ECI, academics and policy

---

100 The European Commission found that in five countries – Cyprus, Denmark, Ireland, Malta and the United Kingdom – citizens would lose voting rights solely by moving abroad. European Commission. "COM (2014/33 final of 29.01 2014. Addressing the consequences of disenfranchisement of Union citizens exercising their right to free movement", 2014. Available from: http://ec.europa.eu/justice/citizen/files/com_2014_33_en.pdf.

101 For more information on "Let-me-vote" ECI go to: https://www.democracy-international.org/eci-let-me-vote-let-us-win.

102 Increasing only from 5,9% on average in the 1994 elections to 11.6% in those of 2009 and then falling back to just over 10% in 2014.

makers there was general agreement that the current disenfranchisement is unacceptable. Four theoretical options were put forward:
- European citizens retain full voting rights in their country of origin;
- They acquire such rights in their country of residence after a certain number of years;
- All European citizens of voting age have a choice between 1 and 2;
- European citizens should have a fair opportunity of acquiring the nationality of the Member State of their residence if they wish to vote there. [103]

Which option to adopt is not self-evident and opinions are divided reflecting different views about the relationship between European and national citizenship and the state of the European Union, whether federal or more intergovernmental. Whilst the European Commission might have been expected to have advocated the third option of choice, as is the case for existing political rights, the Institution in fact advocates the more national, less European, first option (Com (2014)38 final). It ought to be possible to retain one's right to vote in national elections in one's country of origin, but if one so chooses to be able to vote in one's country of permanent residence.

Would this gap be filled by the European Union becoming a party to the ECHR? The European Court of Human Rights has so far rejected appeals by expatriates noting that they are less concerned by the day-to-day problems back home, even though "new technologies and cheaper transport has enabled migrants to maintain a high degree of contact with their state of nationality." Such practical considerations must be weighed against the general principle also highlighted by the Court that: "the right to vote is not a privilege. In the twenty-first century, the presumption in a democratic state must be in favour of inclusion."[104] The "Let –me-vote" campaign needs more support since public and political opinion remains highly divided on extending political rights not just on the basis of nationality, but also residence. Moreover, full political rights for European citizens must mean the possibility to vote not only in national elections, but also regional elections and referenda in their country of residence.

---

103 Baubeck, R., Cayla, P., Seth, C. "Should EU citizens living in other Member States vote there in national elections?" EUI Working Papers, RSCAS 2012/32, EUDO Citizenship Observatory, European University Institute, 2012.
104 Judgement of 7 May 2013 in the case of Schindler v. the United Kingdom.

(iii) *Extending European citizenship to legally resident third country*
      nationals in the Union

For many, the issue is not just how European citizens can acquire full political rights, but who is a citizen in the first place. When European citizenship was introduced in the Maastricht Treaty, the main criticism from
human rights organisations and those defending immigrants and asylum
seekers was that it was based on nationality rather than residence, thus excluding 21 million third country nationals living legally in the EU. The
only way to achieve European citizenship is by becoming a citizen of a
Member State, but a declaration attached to the Maastricht Treaty states
that "the question whether an individual possesses the nationality of a
Member State shall be settled solely by reference to the national law of the
Member State concerned."[105] The problem is that it is much easier to become naturalised in some countries than others. There are different arguments in favour of a more inclusive approach to European citizenship.

On principle, as long as those who do not have the nationality of a
Member State but are legally resident in the Union do not have Union citizenship, they are more likely to suffer discrimination. Opposition may be
formidable but removing where possible the distinction between citizens

---

105 Anyone looking for confirmation that European citizenship could with political
    will be obtainable should review the EUDO debate (*"Should European citizen-
    ship be for sale?, "The Maltese Falcon, or: my Porsche for a Passport!"*). As
    Ayelet Shachar explains kicking off the debate: "Consider the following exam-
    ples. Affluent foreign investors were offered citizenship in Cyprus as "compensa-
    tion" for their Cypriot bank account deposit losses (the value of which was set at
    €3M in the aftermath of the EU bailout). In 2012, Portugal introduced a "golden
    residence permit" to attract real estate and other investments by well-to-do indi-
    viduals seeking a foothold in the EU. Spain recently adopted a similar plan. On
    12 November 2013, Malta approved amendments to its Citizenship Act that put
    in place a new individual investor legal category that will allow high-net-worth
    applicants to gain a "golden passport" in return for €650,000. Under these cash-
    for-passport programmes, many of the requirements that ordinarily apply to those
    seeking naturalisation, such as language competency, extended residency periods
    or renunciation of another citizenship, are waived as part of an active competi-
    tion, if not an outright bidding war, to attract the ultra-rich." Malta's policy was
    condemned by the European Parliament, which in a resolution adopted on 16 Jan-
    uary 2014 "underlines the fact that the rights conferred by EU citizenship are
    based on human dignity and should not be bought or sold at any price." The
    scheme with some modifications appears to have been accepted however by the
    European Commission as not contrary to European law.

and denizens is an effective way to combat racism and xenophobia. Such an initiative would also underline the Union's commitment to a citizenship regime based on equal treatment and non-discrimination. Moreover, European citizenship has been placed now in the broader framework of the Charter of Fundamental Rights with its promise of equalisation of rights for everyone in the EU.

In economic terms, there appears little logic in a European labour market composed of increasingly mobile European citizens, whilst legal immigrants are locked in national markets. Particularly if progress can be made towards common external borders, genuine freedom of movement within the Union should become a realistic option. A more global approach to intra-EU migration is advocated with companies able to recruit on the European market before looking overseas.[106] Creating a European labour market of which third country nationals should be a part is seen by most economists and the European Commission as a way to help absorb asymmetric shocks, particularly in the Euro zone. If economic arguments are not sufficiently convincing, there is also the case for greater social inclusion.

In practical terms, the two groups of migrants can find themselves in the same situation paying taxes, sending their children to the same schools and using the same services. Member States have also made progress with the equalisation of political rights for third country nationals with those of European citizens. The EU regime for coordination of social security arrangements has been extended to third country nationals who can also benefit if recognised as long-standing migrant workers from the right to seek work in another Member State. The gap is closing at least on paper. Where situations are similar between citizens and non-citizens, the tendency should be to make the process of naturalisation easier.[107] Giving the same citizenship status to everyone legally resident in the EU would remove one of the main barriers to the exercise of free movement rights for European citizens with third country national family members or partners.

In the past, the European Parliament endorsed a policy it no longer defends, of extending European citizenship to third country nationals who

---

106 See for example: Dhéret, C., Lazarowicz, A., Nicoli, F., Pascouau, Y., Zuleeg, F. *Making progress towards the completion of the single European labour market.* EPC Issue Paper no. 75, European Policy Centre, May 2013.

107 The EUDO observatory already referred to includes a wealth of information on different regimes and procedures for acquiring citizenship.

have more than five years legal residence. In a changing political climate, the EU has resorted to second-order measures. Its key reform which in theory grants free movement rights to work in another Member State to long term third country residents has not been used.[108] This is because the Member States have not provided enough information about this possibility and can put up barriers to its application. Other second-order measures such as the "Common Basic Principles on Immigrant Integration Policy in the European Union"[109] or the European integration fund have been incorporated by the Member States in their own policies and to an extent nationalised. The communities of third country nationals appear to have lost some sense of a common European future. For that to be restored there should be a return to the statement made by the Tampere European Council in October 1999 whereby "The European Council endorses the objective that long-term resident third country nationals be offered the opportunity to obtain the nationality of a Member State in which they are resident."[110] There is no doubt that the legally binding Charter of Fundamental Rights reinforces that statement.

Finally, there is a risk that a more inclusive European citizenship within the Union could co-exist with a common immigration policy and external borders becoming a fortress Europe. Policies of visa liberalisation for countries bordering on the EU have been successful in the case of the Balkans for example and should continue, as proposed in the attached guidelines. At the time of writing, it is likely that visas will no longer be required for Turkish citizens travelling to the EU.

---

108 "The weak impact...is to be deplored." European Commission. *Commission report on the application of Directive 2003/109/EC concerning the status of third country nationals who are long-term residents (COM (2011)585 final) of 28.9.2011.*, 2011. Available from: http://ec.europa.eu/dgs/home-affairs/what-we-do/policies/pdf/1_en_act_part1_v 62_en.pdf.

109 See "The Common Basic Principles for Immigrant Integration Policy in the EU" available from: http://www.eesc.europa.eu/resources/docs/common-basic-principles_en.pdf and "Press release 2618th Council Meeting Justice and Home Affairs Brussels, 19 November 2004" available from: http://www.consilium.europa.eu/ueDocs/cms_Data/docs/pressData/en/jha/82745.pdf.

110 "Tampere European Council 15 and 16 October 1999". See: http://www.europarl.europa.eu/summits/tam_en.htm.

CHAPTER 6 How can involvement and access of citizens to the European Institutions be made more effective?

Certainly the seasoned traveller looking for the EU Institutions in Brussels would not find the expected cross-section of the European population going in and out of their prestigious buildings. How can access for citizens and their involvement in the European Institutions be made more effective?[111] So far the EU Institutions have gone further with a rights agenda than other aspects of citizenship. The introduction of Union citizenship did though seek a balance between rights and improved means of access to the EU. The Maastricht Treaty formalised the right to petition the European Parliament and created the post of European ombudsman. The first right of European citizens is freedom of movement within the European Union, whereas procedures and channels of communication creating a link between them and the European Union Institutions are a much later addition.

As pointed out in chapter 4, the European citizen finds at European level similar channels of complaint and ways to make his or her voice heard as at the national level. The question arises of why more use is not made of these mechanisms by citizens?[112] Petitions can be effective, for example where they are based on evidence of infringements of European law which can be followed up by members of the European Parliament with the Commission and national authorities. It can be argued that the petition procedure is too slow to be really useful, but it is an effective way of backing up a complaint. Similarly, especially collective petitions, sometimes signed by hundreds of thousands of European citizens, are a way of setting

---

111 A typical Monday morning in the European quarter of Brussels: 9 a.m. delegations of lobbies and interest groups start arriving for appointments with Commission officials at the "Berlaymont". 9.30 a.m. experts show their invitations as they go through security at the Borschette conference centre. 10 a.m. lobbyists show their passes which are validated at the reception desk in the European Parliament. At 11 a.m. a coach load of citizens is shepherded to the visitors' centre and makes a tour of the Institutions (without disturbing the corridors of power) and returns home after lunch with a collection of brochures.

112 The annual reports of the Petitions Committee and the European ombudsman provide statistical evidence, examples and success stories. See also the table below.

an agenda and supporting the case for European legislation. At its monthly meetings, the Petitions Committee hears selected delegations of petitioners and can sometimes advocate effectively for their cause.

In a similar way, the European ombudsman is an independent EU body, on the side of the citizen. The current ombudsman, Emily O'Reilly sees her role certainly as an advocate for the citizen. The European ombudsman can act on the basis of complaints or on her own initiative:

Complaints: The main obstacle for citizens lies in the mandate of the ombudsman, restricted to complaints against maladministration in the EU Institutions, whereas most problems they encounter lie with the failure of national administrations to implement EU law correctly. Some 70% of complaints to the European ombudsman are inadmissible. To deal with the frustration, a holistic approach is attempted: a network of national ombudsmen has been created and the website helps citizens find their way to the right interlocutor.[113] Where complaints are admissible, the procedure is effective, but places a heavy burden on citizens who have to argue their case as effectively as the EU Institutions when they defend their position. Recommendations by the European ombudsman are not legally binding, but have sufficient moral authority to become implemented.[114]

Own Initiative inquiries: The impact of the European ombudsman taking initiatives is evident on all the issues described in this chapter to improve transparency and governance in the EU Institutions. The Maastricht Treaty introduced transparency and access to documents, but only as a non-binding declaration (no. 17). Thanks to an own-initiative inquiry by the European ombudsman, EU Institutions and agencies (except the CJEU and the European Central Bank) followed a recommendation to introduce access to documents in their internal rules of procedure. This amplified the impact of the declaration. Together with the case law of the CJEU, the European ombudsman contributed to the inclusion of access to documents in the Treaties when they were next revised in Amsterdam and was an active participant in the debate in the process of drawing up the legislation.

---

113 For more information on European Ombudsman go to: http://www.ombudsman.europa.eu/home/nl/default.htm.

114 Thanks to an ECAS complaint the Commission released documents relating to the UK and Polish opt-outs to the Charter of Fundamental Rights, for example. The process was however too time consuming and technical for any normal citizen.

NUMBER OF REQUESTS FOR ACCESS TO DOCUMENTS, PETITIONS AND COMPLAINTS IN YEARS 2010-2013.[115]

Requests for access to documents:	2010	2011	2012	2013
European Parliament	1139	1161	777	610
European Council	9 188	9 641	6 166	7 564
European Commission	6 127	6 055	5 274	5 906
Petitions to European Parliament	1746	2091	2322	
Complaints to Ombudsman	2727	2544	2460	2415

In this chapter, we examine separate processes to bring the EU Institutions closer to the citizen: access to documents, transparency in lobbying and public consultations. These processes have been driven by three main factors. The first was enlargement of the EU to the Scandinavian countries which created a pro-transparency minority in the Council in favour of Treaty reform and greater access to documents – now a group of just four: (Sweden, Finland, Denmark and the Netherlands).[116] This group gained support from the European Parliament, the European ombudsman and the case-law of the European Court against an indifferent or mildly hostile majority.[117] Secondly, the European Council has to an extent built on the earlier historical trend described in chapter 1, and been sympathetic to calls not so much for a right of access for the public, but for better communication towards the public and a peoples' Europe. Alongside access to documents, demands to open up the secretive legislative decision-making process in the Council of ministers were successful, and it is here that most progress has been made. A third factor and driver of reform was a

---

115 Data taken from the following documents: ''Report from the Commission on the application in 2014 of Regulation (EC) No 1049/2001 regarding public access to European Parliament, Council and Commission documents'', ''European Ombudsman: Annual Report 2014'', ''2013 Annual Report of the European Parliament on Public Access to Documents (Regulation (EC) No 1049/2001 – Article 17)'' and *"Council Annual Report on Access to Documents"*. See also "Public Access to Documents 2014: Bureau Contribution to the European Parliament's Annual Report" (2014).

116 Hillebrandt, Z. M., Curtin, D., Meijer, A. 'Transparency in the EU Council of Ministers: An Institutional Analysis.' European Law Journal, Vol. 20, No. 1, pp. 1-20, January 2012. DOI: 10.1111/eulj.12051.

117 Civil society groups have also played a role: Statewatch, the International Federation of Journalists and environmental groups in particular.

Commission white paper on European governance following an intensive review and consultation process in 2001.[118] It is however immediately apparent that the pro-transparency coalition within and outside the Institutions is fragile, and ultimately needs to show permanent support including from citizens themselves coming forward in greater numbers. Periodic opportunities offered by the door being opened for Treaty and governance changes are insufficient. This is again an area where strengthening European citizenship requires more continuous input across a broader spectrum of civil society movements. Access to documents, greater transparency in lobbying and open consultations are examined below. By bringing them together, it becomes apparent that improving their use by citizens requires similar improvement in each case.

(i) From access to documents to freedom of information

Progress has been made towards more openness since the non-binding declaration was added to the Maastricht Treaty in 1993, which when the Treaties were next revised at Amsterdam in 1997 became a right of access to documents, put into effect by regulation 1049/2001.[119] The initiative by the European ombudsman to persuade all institutions and agencies to adopt codes of conduct in their internal rules gave citizens the possibility to appeal internally against refusals to provide the documents requested and if necessary externally to the European ombudsman or Court of Justice. It was this earlier practice which was reflected in the regulation.

There are still however areas such as "trialogue" meetings between the Council of Ministers, European Parliament and Commission in the first reading of legislation, which remain a paperless "black hole". Access to documents relating to negotiations with countries outside the European Union, such as the current negotiations with the US on the transatlantic trade and investment partnership (TTIP) – is also closed, leading to many protests during the European election campaign and a recent citizens' ini-

---

118 See "COM(2001) 428 final on European governance - white paper", 2001. Available from: http://eur-lex.europa.eu/legal-content/EN/TXT/?uri=URISERV%3Al10109.

119 Regulation (EC) No 1049/2001 regarding public access to European Parliament, Council and Commission documents. See: http://www.europarl.europa.eu/RegData/PDF/r1049_en.pdf.

tiative (STOP TTIP). Despite a recent ruling by the Court of Justice of the European Union in the Access info case (Case C-280/11 of 17 October 2013) the Council is still reluctant to publish the names of national delegations. This creates a barrier to being able to act as a European citizen since it is impossible to know how one's own government negotiates in Brussels. In 2012 negotiations broke down between the European Parliament and Council of Ministers on Commission proposals for reform of Regulation 1049/2001. This proposal would have restricted the right of access to documents, by defining more narrowly what is meant by a document. To reduce the gap between the often exaggerated claims for transparency and actual practice, reformers have to rely more on complaints and judgements by the European Court than legislative reform, which could result in less rather than more openness. Transparency has yet to be fully incorporated in an administrative culture, where there is still a belief that "transparency kills transparency."

Another way of approaching reform would be to make the access to documents more citizen-friendly, to increase use of the rights which is limited as the table above shows. A certain backlash against greater access can be explained by this apparent lack of interest by citizens. According to a Commission spokesman, most requests to see internal EU documents come from "lawyers from big corporations" and "nutty NGOs" (EU observer 6 June 2012). The majority of requests come from academics, European associations, lobby groups, law firms, consultancies with very few from journalists let alone individuals. A high proportion of requests are sent from Brussels-based organisations, which shows that this has become a tool for insiders. A citizen's right has to an extent become hijacked by organised interests, many of which have privileged access already to the EU Institutions.[120] The proposal made in point 17 of the guidelines in the annex for a right to be informed is relevant. The Institutions have good websites and produce leaflets on access to documents in all languages. What is lacking is a more pro-active communication campaign so that citizens are aware that they have a right to access EU documents in the first place.

---

120 Heremans, T. *Public access to documents: Jurisprudence between principle and practice (between jurisprudence and recast.* Egmont Paper no. 50, Brussels: Academia Press for Egmont - The Royal Institute for International Relations, September 2011.

In the guidelines attached to this book (point 14) it is proposed that there should be a change from an access to documents to a freedom of information system. Under the first, the citizen has to have prior knowledge of the EU and know what documents to look for, which is an unreasonable barrier. Freedom of information implies more of a duty on the part of the administration to help the citizen find the documents actually needed. This can help avoid situations where untargeted requests for documents result in receiving volumes of irrelevant paper work. The European Parliament has called on the Institutions to appoint information officers to assist citizens and ensure respect for deadlines and compliance with the regulation. Moreover, each institution has been obliged under the regulation to set up a register of documents which in the case of the Commission with its decentralised administration, is far from complete. The aim should be that any citizen can easily trace the documents they want in their language, and find out where they come from and the next stage. In the guidelines, it is also proposed that transparency should be extended to inter-institutional negotiations on legislation and trade issues. Such reforms do not necessarily require Treaty changes, or even changes in legislation so much as in practice and administrative culture. This still leaves though the complex and opaque world of interest groups and lobbies outside the EU Institutions.

(ii)   The transparency register: whitewash or the basis for regulation of lobbying?

Whilst the EU legislative process and the Institutions have become much more open, input to the process through lobbying remains the "elephant in the room" or the large problem which remains nevertheless hidden from view. The problem is though becoming more visible as a result of the work of organisations such as Corporate Europe Observatory ("exploring the power of corporate lobbying in the EU") and Transparency International. The public is even offered tours of the organised lobbies in Brussels.[121] The question of codes of conduct or regulation of lobbying is on the agenda in several European countries, as the causes of the financial and economic crisis are unravelled. The European Commission claims that

---

121   Corporate Europe Observatory. See: http://corporateeurope.org/.

in parallel with access to documents and more openness within the public administration, the citizen can now find out who is lobbying the EU, thanks to the transparency register: "We preserved the wide scope of the register which is unique in the world."[122] The transparency register, which began with a modest Commission scheme and which is now jointly run with the European Parliament, has expanded from 2,500 entries by organisations in the 2008 to 7,680 by the end of May 2015 and over 9,000 today. There could be well over 30,000 lobbyists round the EU.[123] The register must make citizens wonder how their voices can compete in such a complex over-crowded environment. The increase in the numbers of EU lobbyists reflects the openness of the institutions, their shifting majorities, expanding agenda and almost certainly a copy-cat phenomenon (ie if "they are there, we had better be there too!"). EU decision-making which is rarely predictable and where there are no inbuilt majorities, is particularly open to lobbying. It is claimed for example that 80% of amendments tabled in the European Parliament come from interest groups.[124] The register does show that funding from the EU budget for civil society organisations contributed a quarter of the total expenditure, and therefore, to more balance and pluralism in lobbying, but corporate interests predominate. From the citizen perspective a "Europe of lobbies is not a proper Europe", especially when the phenomenal growth of this sector is combined with a shrinking presence of accredited media to the EU Institutions.

There is still a long way to go before the footprint of lobbying on the legislative process becomes clear. The register provides the overall picture and a varied amount of detail about specific organisations. It is not though

---

122 Speech by Maros Sefcovic, Commission Vice President on 13 December 2013.

123 Estimate derived from van Schendelen, R. *The Art of Lobbying the EU: More Machiavelli in Brussels.* 4th ed. Amsterdam: Amsterdam University Press, 2013. For a statistical breakdown of the register by categories see annual report by the joint secretariat for 2014. On 31/05/2015, there were 7680 registrants in the register. They are from the following (sub)sections: I – Professional consultancies/law firms/self-empoloyed consultants – 917; II – In-house lobbyists and trade/business/professional associations – 3,883; III – Non-governmental organisations – 1,956; IV – Think tanks, research and academic institutions – 522; V – Organisations representing churches and religious communities – 40; VI – Organisations representing local, regional and municipal authorities, other public or mixed entities, etc. – 362.

124 Rasmussen, M. K. *Lobbying* the *European Parliament: A Necessary Evil. CEPS Policy Brief No. 242.* May 10, 2005.

possible to know, by consulting the register, which organisations are lobbying the EU Institutions on which specific issues and with what resources. The studies referred to point to a number of shortcomings:

- Coverage is by no means complete with many financial lobbyists such as Standard & Poors, City of London Corporation or Credit Suisse missing. Also missing are leading international law firms which have to register in the United States, but not under the EU regime, major corporations and still some consultancies.
- There are still failures by some lobbyists to declare who are their clients, whilst financial reporting is particularly unreliable, with some organisations under-reporting, others declaring their total turnover.
- There is often a discrepancy between the number of lobbyists from a given organisation who have access passes to the European Parliament and the number actually declared.
- Entries are often vague when it comes to explaining to what legislative processes the lobbying is directed; the preference of organisations is to put forward a general statement of their aims, always in favour of a better, more sustainable world.

Alter-EU claimed in its January 2015 report that "the revamped register currently being launched, will not significantly improve the accuracy of the lobby data... and will not enable any interested person to really know who is lobbying whom, and how much is being spent on lobbying in Brussels."[125] It may be too early however to see what improvements will come from an improved register and a review process which should encourage registrants to be more accurate: they must all now declare their estimated costs related to relevant activities; human resources invested must be broken down, rather than just giving an overall figure; they must declare their participation in EU expert groups and other forums. This is an uphill struggle. The increasingly overcrowded competitive and commercial lobbying sphere is difficult to make transparent.[126] The register does place

---

125 Tansey, R. *New and improved? Why the EU Lobby Register still fails to deliver?* Alliance for Lobbying Transparency and Ethics Regulation (ALTER-EU), 2015.
126 The book by van Schendelen mentioned already stresses the point that lobbying has become much more professional and therefore resource intensive. "Get in early and stay in" is the lesson from ECAS tips for the would-be Euro-lobbyist.

more information in the public domain, but studies suggest that it still falls short of its aim.[127]

In a speech to the European Parliament on 15 July 2014, the incoming President of the European Commission, Jean-Claude Juncker declared he is "committed to enhanced transparency when it comes to contact with stakeholders and lobbyists" and to making the voluntary register mandatory, covering not only the Commission and the European Parliament, but also the Council of Ministers. This statement of intention is proving to be harder to implement in practice than might be immediately apparent since no legal basis has been found to make the register not only binding on the Institutions, but also on the lobbyists and their organisations. Governments tend to argue that lobbying the Council amounts to just lobbying them and should not therefore be subject to the same European rules. There is apparently no intention of introducing a European law which would oblige lobbyists to be fully open, honest and accurate about their activities. Instead, there are two measures in place falling short of a binding requirement:

— *Incentives*: Joining the register is a precondition for organisations and individuals to have a special access pass to the European Parliament. Since late 2014 this incentive has been taken up by the Commission which in principle will only meet with organisations on the register. There is now a requirement that information about high-level meetings between Commission representatives and lobbies should be made public. This is however only the tip of the iceberg as there is no disclosure of the majority of meetings taking place at a lower level in the administrative hierarchy.

— *Spot checks*: These are carried out by the joint secretariat of the register – (some 900 quality checks in 2014 resulting in 212 non-eligible entries being removed) whilst a new 'alerts and complaints' procedure has been introduced.

So far so good, but the register has done more to reveal the problem than solve it. The focus on this issue by the EU has also stimulated initiatives at

---

127 Greenwood, J., Drezer, J. "The Transparency register: A European vanguard of strong lobby regulation?" *Interest Groups & Advocacy*, Vol. 2, pp. 139–162, April 2013. DOI:10.1057/iga.2013.3.
See also Arauzo, E., Hoedeman, O., Tansey, R. *Rescue the Register! How to make EU lobby transparency credible and reliable.* Alliance for Lobbying Transparency and Ethics Regulation (ALTER-EU), June 2013.

national level, particularly in more "latin" countries such as France where "lobbyist" does not even appear in the list of professions. The EU deserves some credit for promoting best practices. Applying such best practices systematically is however a demanding task as the recommendations in a recent report by Transparency International suggest. If the aim is to reveal the "legislative footprint"[128] of lobbying the public needs to see all those involved in the policy-making process and exactly what their role and influence is by standardising the lobbying information and ensuring that it is communicated at the right time. Transparency is an essential first step, but it does not on its own bring citizens into the process, which is why we now turn to the possibilities offered by public consultations. Is this a means to give a voice particularly to those who are not lobbying or do not have a permanent presence close to the EU Institutions? Surely that should be the case.

(iii) Towards a reinforced culture of consultation and dialogue?

In theory, citizens' interests which are not represented by groups round the European Institutions have a chance to be heard by participating in public consultations which are advertised on the Your Europe website.[129] Indeed the Commission communication setting out "general principles and minimum standards of consultation of interested parties by the Commission" (COM/2002/704 final), mentions the need to involve hard to reach or minority interests. In terms of the standards, the Commission opted rightly for an open public approach. The standards require consultation processes to be in clear and precise language, to reach a wide audience, leave enough time to respond (recently extended from 8 to 12 weeks) and provide "acknowledgement and feedback." A wide ranging review process led to the Commission white paper on European governance in 2001, from which the standards emerged. There is nothing wrong with the standards, which in a similar way to the transparency register have influenced national practice. For example in the new Member States, in the reform processes after the end of the communist period, the Commission consultation

---

128 Berg, J., Freund, D. "Legislative footprint: What's the real influence of lobbying?" Transparency International EU Office, 2015.

129 See: http://europa.eu/youreurope/. At the time of writing the Commission is inviting views on the future of the Transparency register.

standards were a clear reference point. Nor are the standards new in the sense that the Commission has always perceived its interest as an unelected institution, to be open, making extensive use of "green papers", hearings, as well as expert groups or consultative bodies. The main purpose of the standards was to upgrade public consultations and make their practice more uniform across the Institution. This has only been a partial success:

— There are still striking paradoxes with examples of "good practice" on relatively soft issues such as the preparation of the legislation on citizens' initiatives (see chapter 7), the input to the "citizenship report", and the failure to involve any wider circle of interests let alone citizens on "hard" issues, such as the legislative proposals in response to the financial crisis. The impact of the standards is uneven.[130]

— The questions asked are in many cases about choices for technical options, which would not make citizens feel they are being addressed (assuming that they spotted the opportunity to respond in the first place) or were being given an opportunity to express their own concerns.

— The greatest entry barrier is the predominance of English only consultations, or the use of only a few languages, despite a recommendation from the European ombudsman in favour of a multilingual regime. Resources are needed for translations. After all, EU citizens have a right to write to the Institutions and receive a reply in their own language.[131]

— The absence of specific individual feedback to participants, even though the Commission usually publishes a report on the results of the process, does not motivate them to put forward their views a second time. This is also a question of putting more resources behind a process which can all to easily become an exercise in ticking boxes, rather than one which can encourage dialogue with citizens and civil society.

— Consultations are on-line processes which are the only cost-effective way to reach a large number of people, but they can appear bureaucratic and impersonal. There should be more opportunity for those who take the trouble to engage to have an opportunity to put their views for-

---

130 For example, a report shows that of 27 different consultations processes relating to legislation and policy in the wake of the economic crisis, most received less than 100 responses coming largely from the financial institutions which had caused the crisis in the first place (see ECAS documents).

131 Article 24 of the Treaty on the Functioning of the European Union (TFEU). Available from: http://eur-lex.europa.eu/legal-content/en/TXT/?uri=CELEX: 12012E/TXT.

ward in a face-to –face dialogue with decision-makers. Public hearings at national or European level are though all too rare and subject to budgetary restrictions.

Public consultations serve a double purpose – first to reach a wider, more diffuse audience than the stakeholders directly affected and thus to improve the transparency and legitimacy of decision-making, and secondly, to gather in more expertise to improve its efficiency. Given the technical nature of EU legislative processes, the second objective has tended to take precedence over the first. This choice in favour of the emphasis on expertise is unlikely to change in the near future. In principle the current priority of the European Commission "better regulation for better results" is a step forward because it seeks to extend hearing from stakeholders earlier than when formal consultation processes are launched and subsequently throughout the legislative process.[132] "The Commission intends to listen more closely to citizens and stakeholders and be open to their feedback at every stage of the process – from the first idea, to when the Commission makes a proposal, through to the adoption of legislation and its evaluation. The Commission intends to establish a web portal where each initiative can be tracked."[133] The aim here is not however to install some permanent dialogue with citizens and civil society for its own sake. The Commission invites factual evidence of the impact of EU rules and the way they are applied by Member States under the slogan "lighten the burden, have your say!" The Communication states "opening up policy-making can make the EU more transparent and accountable" – but it is also an example of the way consultation is used to further the specific interests of the Institution. The Commission is looking for support for its better regulation agenda throughout the decision making process. [134]

This objective has by no means general support. A "Better regulation watchdog" has been set up by a coalition of European NGOs in the environmental, consumer protection and other areas. On 18 May 2015, Monique Goyens of BEUC – the European Bureau of Consumer Unions said:

---

132 European Commission. "Communication from the Commission to the European Parliament, the Council, the European Economic and Social Committee and the Committee of Regions: Better regulation for better results – An EU agenda." COM(2015), Strasbourg 19.5.2015.
133 Ibid.
134 Ibid.

"We observe a lack of willingness from the European Commission to take the measures necessary to protect consumers from unhealthy food, dangerous chemicals in consumer products or to provide for better labelling. Several initiatives have been delayed or are not being pursued anymore. The Better Regulation Watchdog network which unites civil society groups from various sectors is a clear signal to the European Commission not to jeopardise legislation protecting public interest. "[135]

Should the Commission be seeking in any case to consult throughout the decision making process? Would it not be preferable if a duty to consult was established separately for the European Parliament and Council of Ministers, as well as the Member States? The current consultation process is too European Commission centred. The other Institutions and national governments should launch their own consultations when they take up a position on European policy and legislation. This would be in the spirit of Article 11 of the Lisbon Treaty which states in paragraph 3: "The Institutions shall maintain an open, transparent and regular dialogue with representative associations and civil society." This is no longer a responsibility therefore only for the Commission but of the "Institutions". The European Parliament is the most open of institutions, but the extent to which there is consultation on proposals coming from the Commission depends on the draftsman for the report or "rapporteur" and his or her committee. Citizens are not given a specific opportunity to be heard, but have to lobby their MEPs, which is more difficult for them than for organised interests. Sometimes committees in the European Parliament organise public hearings. It is difficult, however, to predict on which issues this will occur, since there is a restriction on the number of hearings allowed. As a result, the dialogue in the European Parliament is far from 'regular'.

In the Council of Ministers, let alone the European Council, Article 11 is yet to be applied. The extent to which the Council relates to stakeholders and citizens depends on the agenda of each country holding the six months presidency. Practises such as conferences organised with stakeholders or delegations meeting the presidency and occasional hearings in meetings of national experts – all such possibilities are used. This resembles, however, a fringe activity organised when it is politically convenient

---

135 Better Regulation Watchdog, press release from 18 May 2015 available from: https://www.etuc.org/sites/www.etuc.org/files/press-release/files/better_regulation_watchdog_network_final.pdf.

rather than a serious and consistent policy for engagement with citizens and civil society. Finally, a serious dilemma for the EU as for any administration is what to do when faced with a crisis. On the one hand, there may be justifiable reasons for not organizing public consultations and lack of time to do so. On the other hand, failure to consult can alienate public opinion and reduce any sense that " we are all in this together". Any semblance of public consultation has been absent from crisis- management by the European Council whether on the Euro, asylum or immigration policy or security threats, thus failing to encourage a European citizen perspective when most needed.

The challenge for the European Union is that opportunities for access are taken up by organised interests rather than the citizens, for whom they are intended. A balance in favour of citizen access has to be restored and not just for an elite who are linguistically competent and have prior knowledge of EU affairs. There is a link between this chapter and chapter 8 with its plea for a European citizenship of greater equality. A basis for many of the reforms described in this chapter was the 2001 white paper on European governance. Is it time for a new white paper? Reforms to achieve more transparency fall into decline over time if they are not revisited and given fresh political impetus. A new initiative is needed which should see citizens as partners and be less centred only on the role of the European Commission-the other Institutions and the Member States should be equally responsible for European governance reflecting the increase in their powers. Another aim would be to bring all these procedures into the 21st century and make use of social media to involve more citizens. As with the incomplete and inaccurate transparency register, the question arises of whether the consultation standards should remain voluntary or become compulsory, at least to ensure that they are more systematic, accessible and published in all official languages. They should also be linked to ways of gathering more input and combined with the processes described in the next chapter for citizen participation.

CHAPTER 7 How to develop European citizenship by strengthening transnational participatory and representative democracy?

How to strengthen participatory and representative democracy, but also a sense of belonging to Europe? Beyond the reforms already described, there remains the challenge of making effective "the right to participate in the democratic life of the Union," which the Lisbon Treaty calls for with its emphasis on participatory and representative democracy.[136] Article 11 paragraph 1 states: "The Institutions shall, by appropriate means, give citizens and representative associations the opportunity to make known and publicly exchange their views in all areas of Union action."[137] Is this just well-worn rhetoric or a statement of serious intent to create a European public sphere? There is no answer yet for the EU Institutions over the last eight years of economic crisis have put the emphasis on output rather than input legitimacy. Even calls for the European Commission to issue a "green paper" on how to implement Article 11 have been resisted.[138] The exception is Article 11 paragraph 4 which required the EU to adopt a regulation to introduce citizens' initiatives.[139] In this chapter, three ways to strengthen transnational participatory and representative democracy are considered: the use of participatory processes, citizens' initiatives and elections to the European Parliament.

---

136 Treaty of Lisbon, 2009. Available from: http://eur-lex.europa.eu/legal-content/EN/TXT/?uri=CELEX%3A12007L%2FTXT.

137 Ibid.

138 Such calls came in particular from the liaison committee with civil society organisations established by the EESC. The Austrian Institute for Law and Policy established in Salzburg carried out a series of consultations and published a report on ways to implement Article 11. See: http://legalpolicy.org/.

139 The problem is legal: Article 11 paragraph 4 (TEU) could be implemented through Article 15 (TFEU), whereas there is no corresponding article in the TFEU for paragraphs 1-3.

(i) Can the participatory democracy toolbox make the EU less remote from citizens?

The answer to this question is a qualified "yes" judging from European-level experiments with participatory techniques carried out in an earlier period. In the wake of the "no" votes to the Constitutional Treaty in 2005 in France and the Netherlands, the European Council called for a period of reflection. Margot Wallström, Vice President of the Commission, proposed a special Plan D for democracy, dialogue and debate (COM (2005) 494 final). Pan-European projects were launched, of which the most significant were "citizen consultations" held in every Member State and at European level, and a large scale European deliberative poll.[140] The projects showed that randomly selected citizens are able to overcome language and cultural barriers, discuss and make recommendations on European issues. To achieve this required setting up a Europe-wide support network and a common methodology. In a follow up communication, the Commission concluded that "these projects showed that the development of participatory democracy on EU-related issues at different geographical levels is possible, both in terms of quality and logistics" (COM (2008) 158 final page 5). Despite the recognition that citizen participatory processes do work at European level, Plan D was terminated with the change in Commission in 2009. Another reason why these practices stopped was because of the onslaught of the economic crisis and costs.[141] This was a shame because one spin-off from the European projects was to encourage national ones, such as the G1000 in Belgium.[142] This crisis also saw a more general trend away from using such techniques to enhance political

---

140 These were organised by Foundation Roi Baudouin and Notre Europe respectively. A report on these and some 100 additional projects were made at the time (*Evaluation of Plan D/Debate Europe citizen consultation projects. Evaluation for the European Commission, DG Communication. Final Report. Version 1.4.*, 2009. Available from: http://ec.europa.eu/dgs/communication/about/evaluation/documents/2009-debate-europe_en.pdf).

141 Questions of cost are too often overlooked. To recruit citizens and host them properly over a weekend, meet travel and hotel costs, provide suitable premises, interpretation and sophisticated IT communication – all this divided across 28 Member States can reach 1 million euro – similar to the cost calculated to collect 1 million signatures for a citizens' initiative.

142 G1000: Platform for democratic innovation: http://www.g1000.org/en/.

participation towards measuring user satisfaction with front-line services.[143]

A wide variety of techniques exist, from assemblies, juries, consensus conferences, to scenario-building exercises. Some are large-scale agenda setting events, others on a smaller scale are designed to examine specific policy dilemmas in more depth. There should be EU-wide citizens' consultations precisely on the development of European citizenship for example. Participatory budgeting, on the other hand, where citizens decide how a proportion of public expenditure should be allocated, would be much more appropriate at a local level. This technique could involve citizens in deciding on the delivery of EU regional and social funds for local community development or how to set up the free movement solidarity fund already recommended.[144] Having a wide choice of techniques is an advantage especially in a multi-level complex structure like the EU. The danger though-especially when funds are lacking - is that almost any meeting with a group of citizens can be passed off as participatory and democratic, even when little attempt is made to carry them out according to accepted methodology. It is important that such practices are based on ground rules, if they are to be taken seriously. Therefore, legislation is necessary particularly on how participants are selected randomly to be representative of the population in terms of age, sex, occupation and place of residence. Standards should also guarantee neutral moderation, equal opportunities for participation, access to expertise, ownership of the final report, engagement with policy-makers and feedback.

These processes are a powerful touch of ancient Athenian democracy where citizens were chosen by lot, and represent ideal conditions of democratic participation. The setting may be different, less formal, but the emphasis on democratic participation in the various "occupy" movements

---

143 This was the new approach taken by OECD which had done pioneering work with its handbook for governments on citizens' information, consultation and participation.

144 For more information about participatory budgeting read Sintomer, Y., Herberg, C., Roecke, A. "Participatory Budgeting in Europe: Potentials and Challenges", *International Journal of Urban and Regional Research*, Vol. 31, No. 1, pp. 164–78, 2008, DOI:10.1111/j.1468-2427.2008.00777.x. See also "How the participatory democracy toolbox can make the European Union less remote from citizens" available from: http://providus.lv/upload_file/Projekti/Eiropas%20politika/2010/Final_Report_EN.pdf.

with their city square assemblies is similar.[145] Much could be learned from the protestors about the renewal of democratic processes.

Before deciding to re-open the participatory democracy toolbox, EU policy makers are likely to ask (apart from cost) three questions: [146]

– *Are citizens sufficiently interested and competent?* Citizens can be trusted to be interested in Europe once Europe shows interest in them. Most admit to initial scepticism before they become engaged, and then show innate knowledge and put forward proposals through the process of engaging with fellow citizens they would not normally meet. These are techniques which encourage new ideas and have a transformative effect on some participants. Citizens do though need good access to experts and the necessary time – which is not always available – to absorb the information they receive and deliberate. EU policy makers are used to input at a high level of expertise, so citizens have to raise their game and they are able to do so.

– *Will EU decision makers really listen?* One of the risks is that the process becomes an end in itself, with not enough emphasis on reaching the right decision makers, thus creating frustration. To change this would require building a citizen participation pillar alongside the consultation processes on specific issues so that the input comes at the right time in the decision-making process, and citizens receive feedback on the extent to which their recommendations were accepted. It is precisely because of the dominance of expertise and lobbying that policy makers have an interest in hearing how their proposals are likely to be perceived by and effect end-users.

– *Are participatory practices sufficiently known to the public at large?* Although there is potential interest from the media in the citizens as unusual participants in European affairs, such practices, even when involving several thousand people across Europe, fail to make sufficient impact. This is another instance of the fragmentation of citizenship policy where those interested in face-to-face deliberation on the one hand and social media on the other, which could produce far wider res-

---

145 Kaldor, M., Selchow, S. ,Deel, S., Murray-Leach, T. "The 'bubbling up' of subterranean politics in Europe." Human Security Research Unit, London School of Economics and Political Science, London, UK, 2012.

146 Similar questions are asked in an article by Carole Pateman titled "Participatory Democracy Revisited." *Perspective on Politics*, Vol. 10, No. 1, pp. 7-19, March 2012. DOI: 10.1017/S1537592711004877.

onance in combination, operate in different circles of interest. One possibility would be to make Europe day on 9 May a major event in the calendar for citizen deliberation. Deliberative and participatory practices should be seen too as a way to support citizens' initiatives, which we consider in the next section.

In conclusion, it is difficult to explain why the EU is not using participatory practices which could help reverse the current trend of dissatisfaction with Europe. It is also a way of connecting to the younger generation for whom such practices come naturally. They would provide more serious evidence for the development of European citizenship than just opinion polls and contribute to creating a European public sphere. The recent crisis-ridden period should be seen as an opportunity to engage with citizens and encourage a European citizen and not just a national citizenship perspective. It is time for a new "Plan D" for democracy.

(ii) Are European Citizens' Initiatives the answer or the illusion of inclusion?

The story after the first four years with the use of European citizens' initiatives (ECIs) is illustrative of a constant theme with the European Union: the gap between intention and practice, showing the difficulty of attempting to encourage citizen participation without having made this first possible by creating a European public sphere.[147] Reforms to bring the citizen closer to the European Union resemble those waves which, far out in the ocean, appear straight and powerful, but which lose strength and shape as they come ashore. The low percentage of successful initiatives raises the question of how well regulation 211/2011 on ECIs is working since it entered into force on 1 April 2012. In autumn 2015, out of 51 proposed initiatives, 31 were registered which represents 61% and from that there are only three successful ECIs, which have passed the one million signatures threshold.[148] Stakeholders are calling for substantial revision of the current structure. "What was originally intended to be a simple and user-friendly

---

147 For an in-depth analysis see: Téglas, P. "The European Citizens' Initiative – (Un)successful Tool of Deliberative Democracy; Present State and Future Perspectives", 2015. Available on ECIT website: http://ecit-foundation.eu/.

148 These are: "Water and sanitation are a human right! Water is a public good, not a commodity"; "One of us" referring to judicial protection of the dignity and right

tool for all EU citizens turned out to be cumbersome and challenging in its use" according to Democracy International which has launched a petition with over 76,000 signatures to save the ECI under the title "Make your voice heard in Europe".[149] Certainly a simpler, more uniform regime for ECIs is desirable, but is this the only reason for failure?[150] It is tempting when legislation becomes difficult to use and implement to place the blame on the legislators themselves, rather than look to wider factors. Regulation 211/2011 was the result of a long process, in which substantial political capital has been invested, and not a European law attributable just to a small group of reformers, so it is not really credible to place all the responsibility for failure on the EU Institutions.

Under Article 11 of the Lisbon Treaty, paragraph 4 on European citizens' initiatives states: "Not less than one million citizens who are nationals of a significant number of Member States may take the initiative of inviting the European Commission, within the framework of its powers, to submit any appropriate proposal on matters where citizens consider that a legal act of the Union is required for the purpose of implementing the Treaties". This provision was included in the Constitutional Treaty in 2004 where the proposal had come from lobbying by the Initiative and Referendum Institute and a specific ECI campaign. It had the support of an MEP in the Convention, Alain Lamassure and an MP Jürgen Meyer, and enough signatures were gathered behind a proposal which succeeded. The introduction of ECIs survived the rejection of the Constitutional Treaty and was taken up in the Lisbon Treaty. Full-scale consultations were carried out by the Commission on the basis of a "green paper" [151] before the draft regulation was presented in March 2010. The hearings organised in the European Parliament both by committees and political groups were a good example of collaboration between civil society organisations leading up to the adoption of the regulation a year later. The European Parliament brought about some simplification of the requirements in the regulation. The Parliament signalled its intention to make this process

---

to life of every human being; "stop vivisection" calling for a phasing out of animal experiments.

149 See Democracy International: https://www.democracy-international.org/.

150 Anglmayer, I. *Implementation of the European Citizens' Initiative: The experience of the first three years.* European Parliamentary Research Service: Brussels, 2015, p. 3.

151 "Green paper on a European Citizens' Initiative COM(2009) 622 final."

open to citizens, not just organised interests, by introducing the idea of a citizens' committee (7 individual European citizens from different Member States) the contact point in the Commission and the hearing in the European Parliament. If the problems can be laid at the door of the legislators, it is not with the EU Institutions so much as with the Member States which insisted on their own requirements for signatures, thus creating 28 different regimes for ECIs rather than a single European one as the Commission had proposed originally. Citizens are still seen as national rather than European, even in the context of European initiatives.

The problems with ECIs certainly reflect wider factors than just the overcomplex formal requirements As Article 11 makes clear, the ECI is not an instrument of direct, but deliberative democracy, allowing citizens to propose a European law within the Commission's competence, but without being able to force the institution, which has the sole general right of initiative, to act. We are not here in the same realm as the Swiss popular initiative in favour of immigration quotas described in chapter 3. The ECI is more than just a petition, as the formal procedures suggest. The intention is that citizens should have the same right as the European Parliament to set the agenda by proposing initiatives. The uncertainty as to outcome, even after 1 million signatures have been collected, is though a deterrent to beginning the process and raising funds. This can be countered by showing that the European cross-border debate has value in itself and can indirectly, if not directly influence the climate surrounding the legislative process. Funders look though for guarantees of tangible result. It is here too that the deeper obstacles, apart from the way the legislation is framed, become apparent.

The community of interest which developed round the legislative process insisted on the need for an information campaign for citizens to become aware of their new right of initiative – a demand which fell on deaf ears. Whilst organisers of ECIs pointed to the difficulty of collecting signatures for a procedure about which people knew nothing, policy makers considered that it was through the process of publicising individual ECIs that the European right of initiative would become better known. In normal times this would have been a reasonable argument. ECIs were however introduced in a climate of crisis, economic recession, rising unemployment and declining European solidarity. With repeated media stories of EU heads of governments locked in crisis meetings over the Euro, Russian threats to Ukraine or migration, could citizens really be expected to take to the ECI in large numbers? Moreover, the ECI is an instrument which sets an agenda to add to the body of EU law. This does not fit well with the Commission's better regulation agenda with fewer new laws being proposed and existing legislation being reviewed, simplified or repealed. Lack of information, a climate of European crisis and no invitation to come forward on the part of the EU – these are the real reasons for the failure of ECIs so far.

At first sight, the requirements for a successful ECI are reasonable. 1 million signatures represents only 0.02% of the total EU population. In the negotiations for the regulation, the minimum number of Member States from which signatures have to be collected was reduced to seven, with the regulation determining the minimum numbers for each. Organisers have to form the "citizens committee" which then seeks registration of the proposed initiative, and if that is accepted by the Commission then has to have an online collection system certified and is allowed 12 months to collect signatures. Once signatures are verified by Member States, the initiative is presented to the Commission and a public hearing held in the European Parliament. In the last stage, the Commission provides an answer as to whether or not it will act on the initiative, or on certain aspects. The regulation is silent on the subsequent steps. Does the citizens committee have a right to be heard on a privileged basis at all stages of the follow-up legislative process, for example? The better regulation guidelines explicitly exclude input from citizens in the context of an ECI. This shows that there is a long way to go before this instrument becomes fully integrated in EU decision-making processes.

The ECI processes nevertheless represent a huge challenge to organisers who have to combine a wide range of skills: knowledge of how the EU works and the issues of legal competence; the capacity to mount and finance a high-profile European campaign; the organising and technical skills to comply with the requirements of the regulation. Much depends on their choice of theme: is the aim of the ECI within EU competence? Is it sufficiently topical and capable of attracting popular media and political support? Does the theme have sufficiently common European resonance across seven countries and more? Can the necessary organisational and financial resources be found? In reality, it is rare to be able to give a positive answer to all these questions and trade-offs are likely. For this reason, the strategic European citizen would be well-advised to consider ECIs, but also alternatives, such as lobbying, petitioning or trying to persuade the European Parliament to ask the Commission to propose legislation. Let us look at these requirements for a successful EU in more detail:

The legal knowledge necessary for the registration of the ECI.

In principle, the regulation provides an open door to the registration of ECIs, because the Commission can only reject initiatives which are "manifestly" outside its competence, frivolous or vexatious. How then to account for the surprisingly high number of refused initiatives: 20 or 41% of the total? Earlier in chapter 4, we have drawn attention to the tension between what interests citizens and the narrow confines of EU competence. On its special web portal for ECIs[152] the Commission provides an explanation of the areas of policy exclusively within its competence, those shared with Member States and those largely in the national domain. General advice is clearly not enough. Some citizens' committees have lacked access to deeper legal analysis both of precedent in their particular area, the case-law of the European Court and the Treaty provisions. At the same time, the Commission's reasons for rejection do not always appear clear and consistent, which has led the European ombudsman to recommend "that the Commission endeavours to provide reasoning for rejecting ECIs that is more robust, consistent and comprehensible to the citizen."[153] There is also pressure too from the European Parliament for the Commission to be more tolerant, by allowing for example that at least part of an ECI could be registered. Some initiatives rejected have provoked mixed reactions, e.g. "Stop TTIP". In at least four cases, citizens' committees have appealed to the Court of Justice (namely "One million signatures for a Europe of solidarity"; "Right to Lifelong Care: leading a life of dignity and independence is a fundamental right"; "Cohesion policy for the equality of the regions and the preservation of regional cultures"; "minority Safe Pack – one million signatures for diversity in Europe"). As so often in the history of the EU, it will be left to the Court of Justice of the European Union to establish the scope and limits of a European citizens' right.

---

152 See "The European Citizens' Initiative. Official Register": http://ec.europa.eu/citizens-initiative.
153 Decision by the European ombudsman closing her own initiative inquiry 01/9/2013 TN points 14-16.

The capacity to mount a high-profile European campaign

In the discussions leading to the adoption of the regulation, one of the concerns voiced particularly by MEPs was that the ECI should become a tool for citizens to join forces across borders, not one to be captured, like other EU reforms, by organised interests and lobbies. The list of initiatives on the Commission's website shows that this danger has been avoided at least partly. Well-entrenched lobbies do not need the ECI and often pursue short-term technical aims, reacting to, rather than proposing new legislative initiatives. To some extent, the ECI process has brought new actors on the European scene, which is surely to be welcomed. Accordingly, it is perhaps not surprising that of these initiatives registered and allowed to go ahead, so few achieved their target of 1 million signatures. And does it really matter that so many were rejected or failed? They did at least show that the ECI can act as a carrier and amplifier of ideas and proposals coming from citizens, and give them more impact than they would have had otherwise. The TTIP initiative, which continued unofficially after being rejected, certainly achieved its objective of awareness raising, collecting over 2 million signatures. In other cases new concerns like "Let me vote" received few signatures but a fair amount of notice. As suggested in the guidelines, it would be desirable to offer an alternative to those ECIs which fall short of the target, for example by giving them a hearing as petitions if they achieve over 100,000 signatures. Such a reform would help to mitigate the disadvantage of the all or nothing approach of ECIs with the risk that those who sign initiatives which do not collect one million signatures being discouraged from participating in European activities in future.

Many organisers distanced themselves, rightly, from the lobbies or organised civil society, but then fell in the trap of believing that their mission was possible or should be, on the basis of a citizens' committee and a basic website in one language. This raised the question of who they were, without behind the committee, some organisations familiar to those being requested to sign. Although with a well-functioning website kept up-to-date and in several languages, it is possible to collect signatures centrally, this requires start-up and running costs of some significance. Not enough information is available on numbers of statements of support collected, but in most cases there is a mixture of signatures on-line and on paper. Collecting signatures face-to-face requires significant presence on the ground with staff and volunteers. More may be needed in countries running into difficulties reaching the threshold. The same issue is unlikely to have equal resonance everywhere. The key factor here is lack of resources and lack of funders, for example among the foundations committed to citizen participation or the particular issue. Organisers have to declare their amount of funding: to say that amounts declared fall short of the estimated 1 million euro required all-in-all to collect 1 million signatures, is a gross understatement. An "Achilles heel" has been an expectation that a new European right should be enforceable regardless and as if by magic, rather than considering that there is a certain responsibility on the part of the European citizen to find the resources to make it work. The active European citizen has to be astute and a good fundraiser.

Organising and technical skills to comply with the requirements of the regulation

In turn, without compliance with the technical requirements of the regulation, even the best run European campaign cannot succeed. In the months following the entry into force of the regulation on 1 April 2012 several ECIs were unable to start. Organisers especially of the first ECI Fratenité 2020 discovered that downloading the free open source software provided by the Commission was difficult and did not solve the problem of setting up a secure system for on-line signature collection (osc). The costs of carrying out the risk assessment, acquiring certification and a secure hosting environment were prohibitive – a budget of at least 20,000 – 30,000 Euros would be needed. The European Commission agreed to "stop the clock" and provided a solution with the use of its own servers to host on-line signature collection for ECIs. This problem should have been foreseen since the Commission, Member States and organisers had one year from the adoption of the regulation to put in place the arrangements for its entry into force. The requirement in 18 of the 28 Member States for citizens to provide an ID number has been identified by organisers as a major obstacle: without it many more people would have signed. The European Data Protection Supervisor concluded that ID numbers were not needed for ECIs. "ECI campaigns have noted significantly more incomplete, inaccurate or aborted support statements in countries that require ID numbers vs. those that do not. This is worst in countries with identity theft problems or histories of state surveillance, such as Bulgaria and Poland.

Citizens of some countries are being frightened away from the ECI"[154]. Data protection requirements under the regulation place a heavy responsibility for organisers to guarantee the security of signatures and also destroy all traces of them after they have been submitted. Finally, apart from the day-to-day work of dealing with technical questions there are the processes of submitting signatures to Member States for verification, and in the final phase liaising with the European Commission and Parliament.

From the experience of the first four years of implementation of the regulation on ECIs, a number of possibilities for reform should be considered. These relate partly to changes in the legislation itself, partly to providing the infrastructure – the European public sphere – in which ECIs can operate effectively. If infrastructure is set up, the question should be asked whether it should apply only to ECIs or could be extended to all channels available for interaction between citizens and the EU Institutions.

The reform of the ECI regulation and its conditions of use should have the following aims:

- Inclusion in the regulation on ECIs of a requirement on the part of the EU Institutions and Member States to launch a communication campaign and inform citizens of their right of European initiative in their own language and in a user-friendly way.
- Clarify the procedure for the legal admissibility test and provide more in-depth advice to citizens' committees so that fewer initiatives are rejected. The acceptance of ECIs which partially meet the admissibility test should be possible after consultation with organisers.
- Propose a simpler uniform requirement for signature collection, name, address, nationality and date of birth being sufficient. The requirement to provide ID numbers should be abolished, given that this is an agenda-setting, not a binding instrument. In the medium term, the proposal in chapter 8 for a European card would be relevant, making it easier to sign on ECI.
- Extend the time allowed for the collection of statements of support from 12 to 18 months, in order to increase chances of success and recognise that awareness raising and organisation for the issue may be easier in some Member States than others.

---

154 See "12 Recommendations in-depth: Eliminate ID number requirements", 4 May 2015. Available from: http://www.citizens-initiative.eu/12-RECOMMENDA-TIONS-IN-DEPTH/.

- Data protection should not prevent organisers from keeping in touch with supporters who agree to this when they sign the initiative.
- Build the supportive infrastructure of a European public sphere, allowing organisers to test their proposed initiatives and benefit from advice. This should include setting up a dedicated European fund for start-up finance provided organisers have insufficient resources and stand a reasonable chance of success. This should be supported by a consortium of funders.
- Create an inter-institutional help desk (cf on the lines of the joint secretariat of the Commission and the European Parliament for the transparency register but extended to EU advisory bodies and civil society help desks) to provide advice for representation, support with a permanent OSC system for initiatives and help with contacts with the European Commission, Parliament and national authorities. Each institution and body would be expected to make a specific contribution to legal, technical and logistical support.[155]
- Innovate by lowering the age to sign or propose a citizens' initiative from 18 to 16 out of recognition that over 70% of signatures come from young people and many concern issues to do with education or popular single issue campaigns which have their support. Moreover, if more emphasis is to be placed on European citizenship education (chapter 8), it has to be practiced, not just taught.[156]

Such proposals are not new and reflect many suggestions put forward by EU Institutions and stakeholders. There has been significant support for a reformed ECI in the European Parliament, but such ideas have met with a cold reception in the European Commission. Only a package of reforms can restore confidence and use of the ECI. In 2011, 22 initiatives were put forward, in 2012, 18; in 2013, 8 and in 2016, 4. At a time when ECIs were a distant hope on the horizon, many observers thought that they could be a way to encourage interest and turnout in the May 2014 European elections. Could political parties campaign to support one or other initiative?

---

155   This proposal owes much to implementation of the European citizens' initiative (The experience of the first three years) European Parliamentary Research Service; Brussels 2015 as well as to the recommendations by the ECI campaign. The idea would be to pool the support. The EU advisory bodies are the European Economic and Social Committee (EESC) and the Committee of the Regions.

156   Ibid. 143, p. 18.

Such an objective will now have to wait until the European elections in 2019.

(iii) How to make elections to the European Parliament more popular and more European?

The complex nature of the European Union as both an intergovernmental and a more supranational structure is reflected in the elections to the European Parliament. The elections are European but largely in name only, with national parties running their own candidates on their own programmes, and when held on the same day as local or national elections, European elections can appear even more second-order. Within the European Parliament, the political groups of the diverse political families operate in a cohesive way, but have limited reach beyond the Institution.[157] The campaign of European political parties with their manifestos which represent a broad consensus can appear marginal and even irrelevant in the context of each country. The process may well be reinforced by the parties and the voters seeing the elections as an opportunity to sanction or support their own government. The picture is by no means simple or uniform. For example, the opposite scenario may well occur when European policy features prominently in a national election. There are also more links developing between the European Parliament and national parliaments which can as a group question the need for a Commission proposal, and are likely to see their role in European affairs strengthened. Dividing lines between national and European politics are not so clear-cut. The European elections are though a sign of the distance between the theory of European political rights, which should be a defining feature of European citizenship, and their practice. In this section, we examine ways to encourage the

---

157 Vote Watch on key votes in 2009-2014 EP, from www.votewatch.eu, shows the results of transnational working together by MPs. "Politics inside the European Parliament is essentially 'democratic' in that it is highly competitive and the coalitions between the MEPs and European parties are based on the left-right dimension of politics, which is the dominant dimension of politics throughout the democratic world. [...] What is missing, however, is a clear connection between this emerging democratic politics inside the European Parliament and how citizens behave in European Parliament elections", from Hix, S. *What's wrong with the European Union & how to fix it*. Cambridge: Polity Press, p. 118-119, 2008.

europeanization of these elections, essential to shifting this transnational political right in the direction of the European citizen.

In the run-up to the European elections in May 2014, the first addressing citizens directly under the Lisbon Treaty, the slogan for the European Parliament's information campaign "Act, React, Impact" was "this time it's different". But to what extent was this really the case? Was there a mobilisation of European citizenry? These were the first elections to provide a verdict of the handling of the economic and financial crisis by the EU. The results revealed the increased fragmentation of public opinion towards Europe, and the tensions between European and national citizenship. Nevertheless, to some extent the elections were different. This suggested that reforms can work and that a basis exists on which to build further to make the elections more European in 2019. The main reason for relative optimism is turnout: in 2014 "the downward trend was significantly stemmed". [158] After the participation rate in European elections dropped from 61.99% in the first election in 1979 to a historically low turnout of 42.97% in 2009, the decline was at least halted in 2014 at 42.54%. This may signal the end of a period where the majority view has been one of scepticism focused largely on issues of turnout.

Declining participation has occurred paradoxically over a period when successive Treaty reforms have increased the powers of the European Parliament, even to an extent where some regard its control of detail in Commission decision-making as excessive.[159] The fact that the Parliament shares legislative power with the Council, representing the governments, has not been enough to persuade voters to turn out in greater numbers. This reflects the lack of information about what the Parliament does. In the complex world of EU decision-making and bargaining among the Institutions, it is also difficult to single out without more information the real influence of the Parliament. The powers of the Parliament are exercised through the process of scrutiny in committee and amendment of Commission proposals to reach a compromise with the Council. It is rare that as an institution it takes a decisive stand, which becomes publicly acknowledged. There may also be a perception that although the powers of the Parliament have increased, real decision-making during the crisis was concentrated in the hands of government leaders in the European Council.

158　European Commission report on the 2014 European elections.
159　Piris, J. *The future of Europe: Towards a Two-Speed EU?* Cambridge: Cambridge University Press, 2011.

Certainly the "legislative footprint" as we have argued in chapter 6 should be made clearer. How much influence does knowledge of the legislative decision-making process have? Levels of voter participation reflect broader issues such as the extent to which it is regarded as a duty to vote, or trust and mistrust in politics, which differs across the Member States (i.e. 76.5% in Belgium where voting is obligatory to 13.1% in Slovakia in the 2014 European elections). Analysis of voter participation reveals another paradox: "Once again, the greatest abstainers in European elections were young people (aged from 18 to 24) and it is they who express the most positive feelings about the EU. Equally worrying is that 54% of respondents found that the European Parliament did "not really take into account the concerns of European citizens. The figure was 41% in 2009".[160] It appears therefore that lack of information about what the European Parliament does, varying degrees of trust and distrust about whether one's vote counts and decline in support for the EU account for an abstention rate of 37%.

For the first time in 2014, the European elections were fought from such opposing standpoints that they appeared almost not as one event, but two: one national and another European.[161]

– The rise of nationalist, eurosceptical parties was predicted in the run-up to the European elections, adding to the traditional concern of low voter turnout. European elections tend to favour smaller parties and a protest vote. The economic and financial crisis imposed cuts and costs on citizens, making the surge of euroscepticism inevitable. The extent of the success of UKIP and the French National Front however exceeded expectation, as did the rise of a number of new, smaller parties taking in all 24% of seats in the European Parliament. The table below shows how at variance with the Charter of Fundamental Rights and values of European citizenship these parties are. It can be argued that there are such significant differences among the eurosceptical minority that they cannot act cohesively. Nevertheless, Marine Le Pen has succeeded in forming a European political group, with all the power and resources that brings.

---

160 2014 post-election survey European elections 2014 Analytical overview European Parliament. Public opinion monitory unit. 27.8% of 18-24 year olds voted, as compared with 51.3% in the 55+ age group.
161 Bertsou, E. The 2014 European Parliament elections: A victory for European Democracy. LSE "Europe in question" Discussion paper series, 2014, p. 31.

Party	Country	Violent?	Hostile to representative democracy?	Extremist past?	Racist?	Xenophobic?	Islamophobic?	Anti-Semitic?	Homophobic?	Sexist?	Democratic contribution?	Direction?
Chrysi Avgi (Golden Dawn)	Greece											
Jobbik	Hungary											
Ataka (Attack)	Bulgaria											
British National Party	UK											
Freiheitlichen Partei Österreichs (Austrian Freedom Party)	Austria											
Slovenská Národná Strana (Slovak National Party)	Slovakia											
Vlaams Belang (Flemish Interest)	Belgium											
Front National (National Front)	France[1]											
Partij Voor de Vrijheid (Party for Freedom)	The Netherlands											
Lega Nord (Northern League)	Italy											
Sverigedemokraterna (Sweden Democrats)	Sweden											
Dansk Folkeparti (Danish People's Party)	Denmark											
United Kingdom Independence Party	UK											
Perussuomalaiset (Finns Party)	Finland											
Fremskrittspartiet (Progress Party)	Norway											
Alternative für Deutschland (Alternative for Germany)	Germany											
Movimento 5 Stelle (5 Star Movement)	Italy											

▇ : high danger ▇ : medium danger ▇ : low danger

– The europeanising innovation of Spitzenkandidaten or lead candidates was the other salient feature of these elections. For some time scholars have suggested that since adding to the powers of the Parliament has not been enough to increase turnout, that what is needed is real political choice, the sense that one's own vote counts in order to elect the executive. For the 2014 elections it was possible to claim "This time it's different", because the Lisbon Treaty states in Article 17 that the results of the European elections should be taken into account when selecting the next Commission President. In order to add substance to that reform each party organisation of the five main political groups offered voters a choice for next Commission President.[162] Whilst imposing the lead candidate met with some resistance from the UK and the governments, in the end they had to recognise that failure to accept the

---

162 Schmitt, H., Hobolt, S, B., Popa, S. A. "Does personalization increase turnout? Spitzenkandidaten in the 2014 European Parliament elections" *European Union Politics*, p. 1-22, 2015.

results would have undermined the promise of more democratic choice. Jean-Claude Juncker duly became Commission President.

This leaves open a number of questions. What will be the influence of the eurosceptical minority in the Parliament? It does result in mainstream parties seeking consensus and a European Parliament where the battle between broadly left and right-wing politics gives way on occasion to divisions between more pro and anti-EU sentiment. Did the innovation of Spitzenkandidaten make any real difference? The article already quoted "Does personalization increase turnout?" concluded that the introduction of lead candidates in 2014 did demonstrate that this pragmatic reform, without altering the electoral system, can make an impact, even though campaigning remained predominantly national.[163] In a resolution of 22 November 2012, the European Parliament "stressed the importance of reinforcing the political legitimacy of both Parliament and Commission by connecting their respective elections more directly to the choice of voters", and the Commission made similar recommendations, "The aim is to transform the nature of elections to the EP by creating a genuine context for the top executive job and a choice between alternative political platforms".[164]

The same article goes on to identify the challenges to meeting such an objective, such as "the lack of an EU wide common public sphere with a common media, not to mention the lack of a common language in which alternative political visions could more easily be discussed." This relates to the broader issues of creating more European citizens in the first place discussed in Chapter 8. Such challenges are not insurmountable, given the necessary resources but the article goes on to point out that the five lead candidates had a total budget of 4.5 million euro (compared to an estimated spending of 2.6 billion U.S. dollars in the last U.S. presidential elections). Another obstacle is the difficulty of nominating candidates with a sufficiently broad European appeal, and in this election the personalities were either new or "insiders", and tended naturally to be recognised most readily in their own countries. Despite the lack of a European public sphere, the Spitzenkandidaten experiment was an encouraging start. At least one of the nine televised debates, with the five candidates, translated in all languages, was seen by 15% of European citizens. The lead candi-

---

163   Ibid.
164   Ibid., p. 4.

dates also travelled extensively around EU-28 and had a significant on-line presence. The analysis already quoted comes to the conclusion that: "individuals who are able to recognise one or more of the lead candidates for the position of president of the European Commission are more likely to turn out to vote in European Parliament elections." This is even more the case if the candidates are seen to be personally engaged in the campaign.

The personalisation of the campaign encourages turnout, but so does the protest vote. There is no doubt that in the run-up to the 2019 European elections, the formula of Spitzenkandidaten should continue – maybe next time with at least one eurosceptical candidate – and ought to be developed, despite resistance by national governments. However, the impact is bound to remain limited and no single reform, at a stroke, can make the elections more European. A more extensive set of reforms should be considered.

– Further develop the 2014 experiment by allowing for more time and resources for the lead candidates to become known across Europe; consolidate the obligation to appoint as President of the Commission the winner of the election.

– Reconsider a proposal made by the Constitutional Affairs Committee in the European Parliament for the introduction of transnational party lists from which 25 MEPs can be elected.[165]

– Although people declared they were marginally better informed before the 2014 elections, continue with information campaigns such as "Act, react, impact".

– As this slogan implies, recognise that top-down information campaigns have limited impact and that a more participatory approach involving civil society organisations is essential to find out what young people in particular expect from Europe and what could motivate them to vote.

– Recognise the variations across Member States and concentrate efforts to increase awareness and participation in those Member States, particularly those that have joined the EU recently where turnout is far below the average.

---

165 Duff, A. *Post-national democracy and the reform of the European Parliament*, Policy Paper No. 42, October 2010. Available from: www.notre-europe.eu.

- Implement recommendations already made by the Commission to make European citizens more aware of their rights to vote and stand as candidates in European elections in their Member State of residence.[166]
- Also implement Commission recommendations to back up the system of Spitzenkandidaten by ensuring that national parties give more mention and prominence to their European affiliations and platforms; these affiliations should also be mentioned on ballot papers.
- Encourage European political party platforms to support European citizens' initiatives during the next campaign for the European elections, assuming that the regime can be reformed in the meantime to encourage its use.

The scope for reforms to the way European elections are organised has increased because the "Spitzenkandidaten experiment" has shown that they can work. As noted however in the conclusion to a debate held among experts in the academic community: "The question of EU legitimacy cannot rest solely with the European Parliament given the extensive shift in economic powers that took place during the euro-crisis. The quest for democratic victory at European level will be a continuous endeavour, as EU transformations necessitate ever more accountability mechanisms and an increased understanding of citizen engagement with Europe."[167]

This is why the guidelines raise the issue of direct democracy and suggest that the European Parliament should at least study the question of EU-wide referenda.

---

166 Commission report on the 2014 European elections, p. 13. The numbers of citizens registered to vote in 2014 elections in their Member State of residence was 8% on average down from just over 10% in 2009. However, there were more candidates – 170 in 2014 as opposed to 81 in 2009.

167 Bertsou, E. *The 2014 European Parliament elections: A victory for European Democracy.* LSE "Europe in question" Discussion paper series, 2014.

CHAPTER 8 Once found, can Cinderella acquire more universal appeal?

At any level, citizenship comes down to a sense that "we are all in this together". In this chapter the theme is that without a much wider perspective on European citizenship the reforms already considered will fail to reach a mass audience. We consider first the implications of citizenship as a condition of equality. We go on to consider three ways to achieve a more equal European citizenship: a right to be informed and educated for European citizenship, universal access to EU mobility programmes and the need for a civil society coalition to campaign for European citizenship. According to one definition:

> "Citizenship is a condition of civic equality. It consists of membership of a political community where all citizens can determine the terms of social cooperation on an equal basis. This status not only secures equal rights to the enjoyment of the collective goods provided by the political association but also involves equal duties to promote them – including the good of democratic citizenship itself."[168]

This is hard to live up to in practice, even in highly developed democratic communities. The link made between rights and duties goes in the direction of the demand for a more holistic approach to European citizenship in the introduction, which is not a difficult demand to meet, given the political will and necessary consensus. Much more difficult to achieve on a European scale is a citizenship of equality. Europe-in-the-making is polarised between "a small elite minority which has substantially europeanised its networks, self-understandings, and political goals, and a large minority who feel shut out from these benefits".[169] As pointed out in Chapter 3, free movement within the EU is more extensive than the offi-

---

168 Bellamy, R. *Citizenship: A Very Short Introduction.* Oxford, Oxford University Press, 2008.
169 Recchi, E. et al. *The Europeanisation of Everyday Life: Cross-Border Practices and Transnational Identities among EU and Third-Country Citizens. Final Report,* EUCROSS, June 2014. Available from: http://www.eucross.eu/cms/index.php?option=com_content&view=article&id=8:the-eucross-project&catid=14:home&Itemid=160.

cial statistics suggest. The practice covers networks in branches of the public administration, local authorities, trade associations in all sectors but also civil society organisations, schools, universities and circles of interest among researchers. There is still though a rough divide between insiders and outsiders, as shown by Eurobarometer polls. A sense of feeling European is higher among young people and those that are better off, whilst over a third of the population has no such feeling.

Part of the answer to progress towards a citizenship of more equal opportunity is the reform agenda at European level. There is though a discrepancy between reforms often seen with high rhetoric as contributing to the legitimacy and accountability of the Institutions and how they fail to engage with a critical mass of citizens. As one author puts it: "procedural changes in the way the EU works, such as increases in the powers of the European Parliament, greater transparency of EU decisions, involving interest groups and national parliaments in EU decision-making and the Charter of Fundamental Rights, have all failed to engage citizens in EU politics."[170] His analysis is that there is not enough incentive for people to engage: "What is missing is the substantive content of democracy: a battle for control of political power and the policy agenda at the European level." It is tempting to focus on what could be a strong pull factor such as genuinely European elections to the European Parliament.

On the other hand, "making EU citizens…requires attention to be paid at all levels of governance to issues of citizenship in general."[171] Reforms within the EU Institutions "will fail to register with Member State nationals if they have not first become more active citizens and self-conscious inhabitants of a European public space." To summarise what this author thinks is required: "first, further socialisation of Member State nationals may in fact be a necessary precondition for, rather than a fortuitous result of citizens' engagement", "second, far more education about the European Union and its policy processes is vital, so that those citizens who wish to advance or block particular policy objectives are able to understand when, why and how to do this…" "third, all actors seeking to breathe life into

---

170 Hix, S. *What's Wrong With the European Union and How to Fix It*. Oxford: Polity Press, 2008.

171 Warleigh, A. 'Making Citizens from the Market? NGOs and the Representation of Interests.' in *Making European Citizens: Civic Inclusion in a Transnational Context*. ed. by Bellamy, R., Castiglione, D., Shaw, J. Basingstoke: Palgrave Macmillan: pp. 118-133, 2006.

EU citizenship for either normative or instrumental reasons must develop reflexive practices which view participatory governance as both means and end."

In order to create European citizens and give European citizenship more universal appeal three sets of reforms appear necessary, beyond the limited impact of reforms in EU Institutions:

– First, a series of proposals for equal access to information, educative and practical experience of Europe. In order for more citizens to be able and willing to participate, for example in European elections, they need to be informed in the first place. But will more information work on its own without the necessary civic education? And in turn would more equal spread of education for European citizenship really work if there was not more equal access to its practical benefits?

– Secondly, hence, the demand for a universal European citizenship entitlement to access a European life-long learning exchange programme at some time in one's life; a special card would guarantee such an entitlement and other European rights of free movement and participation.

– Thirdly, could there be a civil society movement for European citizenship? It is self-evident that to a greater extent than citizenship at a local level, the individual is relatively powerless. This is why a more collective approach to putting forward complaints, petitions and making European citizens' initiatives work is essential. Governments have been stronger advocates for European citizenship before than after its inclusion in the Maastricht Treaty; over the next generation the challenge to develop European citizenship should be taken up by civil society.

(i) Should there be a right to be informed and educated for European citizenship?

A right to be informed

A right to be informed is the gateway to citizenship as the right to have rights, and in particular when dealing with a distant Europe, almost a precondition for European citizenship as an equal status. If you do not know what your rights are in the first place, how can you exercise them? Knowledge of European rights has improved, but awareness remains limited to under 50% of the population with averages obscuring large national and socio-economic differences. Over time unequal access to knowledge of European rights has tended to increase with a minority of citizens on the move asking far more complex questions about European law in relation to their social entitlements on professional qualifications, the majority having limited or no knowledge. It is therefore proposed in the guidelines attached to this book that "all citizens of the Union, and all natural persons residing in a Member State, shall be informed about their European rights and the activities of the Union." This would place obligations not only on the EU Institutions, but also on the national governments to provide clear, objective information in all languages. The guidelines recommend, by way of example, "to give every European citizen of voting age a handbook about European rights and how to find out more about the European Union."

The idea of a right to be informed was first proposed in 2003 before the start of the Convention on the Future of Europe and promoted by civil society organisations and think tanks.[172] If the idea was not taken up by the Convention, it at least gained the support of the European Parliament and also the Commission which in its own proposals for Treaty reform turned a citizens' right into an obligation on the part of the Institutions to provide information. In reality, the proposal supported efforts by the European Commissioner responsible, Margot Wallström, to make listening to citizens and two-way communication a policy in its own right. Some of the structures to meet such a right were put in place. A more coherent set of priorities decided on the basis of an inter-institutional agreement between the Commission, the European Parliament and the Council; a "one-stop shop" for information and advice has been set up on the Europa website. There is also greater decentralisation towards EU offices and "public spaces" in most Member States. By working together, the Institutions could make more impact. Efforts to communicate Europe are still open to the criticism that they aim more to sell or justify EU activities than meet the information needs of all citizens. Despite this, progress has been made to create the delivery mechanisms to meet such an objective at least by the EU Institutions. Significant efforts are though necessary on the part of Member States which should be under an obligation to inform citizens about their rights and European policies.

---

172 Upson, R. *Connecting with Citzens,* ECAS, 2006, available at http://www.ecas.org/wp-content/uploads/2014/11/2006_ Connecting-with-Citizens_Does-the-EU-have-the-will-to-tackle-its-information-deficit.pdf.

A right to be informed should be considered as a realistic option, when the Treaties are next revised, because of the steps taken since the time when this was first suggested. A clearer legal basis for communication strategy could encourage more resources for a multi-media, multi-lingual approach to creating a European public sphere. On its own however, Treaty reform is not enough. There has to be clear political leadership. That is why the guidelines call for the appointment of a senior European Commissioner "with responsibility for communication and all aspects of Union citizenship."

A right to European citizenship education

Even if information about the EU and European rights became more universally available, how much would it really mean to people who had received absolutely no previous education or grounding in the subject? Providing the educational background is a vast enterprise, but in theory a possible one because of the recent spread of citizenship education across Europe, which has been something of a silent revolution. The movement has been similar in different countries and does reflect common concerns:

– One concern certainly is based on evidence of a decline in voter turnout, membership of political parties and voluntary organisations, lack of interest in taking part in school activities, let alone the wider community. Linked to this, students need to be more broadly equipped with general knowledge to counterbalance the pressure for increasing specialisation.
– Another concern was filling the vacuum after the fall of the Berlin wall in 1989 which presented the challenge of replacing old regimes with new institutions and processes to underpin democracy. Democracy has to become an essential aspect of daily life, not just a system of government.
– In more complex multi-cultural societies, citizenship education is seen as a defence against the rise of violence, racism, extremism, xenophobia, discrimination and intolerance.[173]

---

173 Georgi, V. B. (ed.) *The Making of Citizens in Europe: New Perspectives on Citizenship Education.* Bonn: Bundeszentrale fur politische Bildung, 2008.

The 47 nation Council of Europe has taken the lead, starting in 1997 and culminating in a European Year of citizenship through education in 2005 and a "Charter on Education for Democratic Citizenship and Human Rights Education" adopted by all Member States of the European Union in 2010.

For the European Year of Citizens in 2013, a special study showed that there is some convergence in understanding about what constitutes citizenship education.[174] It encompasses the old and narrower concept of "civic education" about formal understanding of the workings of democratic institutions, to embrace a concern that young people should become active citizens. According to the study "citizenship education is commonly understood to include four main aspects: (a) political literacy; (b) critical thinking and analytical skills; (c) attitudes and values and (d) active participation." Translating such objectives in the curricula results in a certain degree of convergence across countries as to the subject matter actually taught, with some limited emphasis on the international and European dimension. There is a tendency for these four objectives to become more prominent in national curricula, and for the subject to become compulsory and included at all levels of education.

This, is however a very superficial generalisation, which only goes to affirm that most countries approach the subject from a similar starting point. The Eurydice study shows how difficult it is to evaluate the extent of citizenship education. One reason is that much is left rightly to the discretion of individual teachers out of respect for academic freedom. There is a rough division between countries which treat citizenship education as a separate stand-alone subject, and those which also or as an alternative approach see it as integrated and cross-cutting in other areas. It is very difficult therefore to compare countries with such different approaches in practice. Where citizenship is taught as a separate subject, the number of years in which it is taught can vary enormously between 12 in France to just 1 in Bulgaria.[175]

It is also very difficult to have any precise idea of how much the European or international dimension is seen as relevant or receives any emphasis. In a much more turbulent economic climate with high youth unem-

---

174 Eurydice. *Citizenship Education in Europe.* Brussels: Education, Audiovisual and Culture Executive Agency, 2012. Available from: http://eacea.ec.europa.eu/education/eurydice/documents/thematic_reports/139EN.pdf.

175 Ibid.

ployment, there is for example, more emphasis on educating young en-trepreneurs than citizens. Nevertheless, one scholar takes an optimistic line:

> *"European policy discussions have shifted considerably in a short period of time. Where in the past citizenship (or at least education for European citizenship) tended to be defined predominantly in terms of identities, cultures and histories, the policies that emerged after 1992 instead tend to depict citizenship as a multifaceted and largely post-national concept. For example, rights – be they civil, political, social, economic, cultural or human – are now deemed to be the cornerstone."*[176]

The same author does though point out that "the reframing process pro-duces a wide range of interpretations of what European citizenship should be, and undermines the possibility of creating a pan-European consensus on what European citizenship really means for its citizens, thus defeating what is arguably one of its central functions." This is similar to the case for a holistic European citizenship argued in the introduction. The Euro-pean Commission has limited competence in the area of education but could use its competence in the area of Union citizenship, to propose after widespread consultations with the teaching profession, civil society and ministries of education, a basic model curriculum for teaching European citizenship. The holistic approach and the guidelines attached to this book may encourage such a process.

As pointed out above, citizenship education may be taught as a self-standing subject or linked to others. For European citizenship education, the two most relevant subjects are European languages and history. The European Commission is able to promote language learning and linguistic diversity as a European objective, especially since governments have en-dorsed a policy of "teaching at least two foreign languages from a very early age."[177] The percentage of pupils learning 2 or more foreign lan-guages has increased on average from 47% in 2005 to 61% in 2010 and the Commission proposes 75% by 2020. There is some progress with the

---

176 Keating, A. "Educating Europe's citizens: moving from national to post-national models of educating for European citizenship." *Citizenship Studies,* Vol. 13, No. 2, pp. 135-151, 2009. DOI:10.1080/13621020902731140.
177 European Council meeting of 15-16 March 2002 in Barcelona.

younger generation, but the gaps between countries are striking, as the table below suggests.[178]

There is evidence that language teaching and citizenship education can reinforce each other. "Much of the literature indicates that, by developing an understanding and appreciation of other ways of life, the intercultural aspect of language teaching makes an essential contribution to education for democratic citizenship".

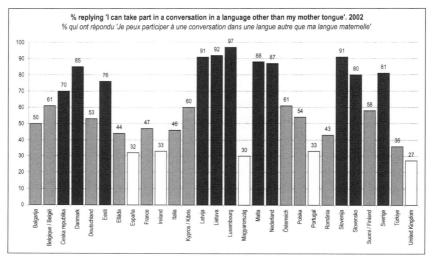

Commission of the European Communities. *The European Indicator of Language Competence.* COM(2005) 356, 1 August 2005.

By comparison with language teaching, where a role for the European Commission is recognised, the teaching of history remains in the strict competence of Member States. It is not surprising therefore that the Union has limited its focus to the twin tyrannies of the 20th century, Nazism and Stalinism. The holocaust is certainly the clearest of all common European memories with its warning of "never again". It could be said that European citizens have a duty of remembrance, especially since the last survivors of the concentration camps are dying. The duty to remember is re-

---

178 See also First European Survey on Language Competences (ESCL). Available from: http://ec.europa.eu/languages/library/studies/executive-summary-eslc_en.p df.

flected in the national laws against holocaust denial. "The Union is an area of shared values, values which are incompatible with crimes against humanity, genocide and war crimes, including crimes committed by totalitarian regimes."[179] It is because of their own past that Europeans have pioneered a right of interference in the affairs of other states for humanitarian purposes or to prevent such crimes. The 2004 enlargement of the Union has added a broader approach and a more complex one to the notion of collective European memory and the totalitarian past of all Member States, especially because of the period when Eastern and Western Europe lived under different regimes. Therefore holocaust memorial day on 27 January has been followed by 23 August as Remembrance Day of the victims of both Nazism and Stalinism.

But to what extent are these memories really the same? What about the North and the South of Europe or crimes committed in the name of colonialisation and empire? The rise of anti-semitism, xenophobia and in particular islamophobia since the terrorist attacks of 11 September 2001 shows that the lessons of the past have not been learned. Should European citizenship be based only on the memories of the 20th century and ignore everything that went before? "Your past is our past" is still not a reality in the European Union[180] and is the last piece in the jigsaw of building a European citizenship which might one day be put in place. It is precisely because European citizenship does not rest on common memories that it needs to invent a common framework. There is a gap where historians might have attempted a history of European citizenship, which they tend to see as a recent phenomenon.

(ii) Could access to EU mobility programmes be more socially balanced and universally accessible?

In the previous sections, it has become clear that the European Union, despite limited powers and resources in these areas, has recognised the im-

---

179 The Stockholm programme adopted by the European Council on 10/11 December 2009 OJC 115 of 4.05.2010.

180 European Commission. "The memory of crimes committed by totalitarian regimes in Europe (COM(2010) 788 final of 22.12.2010 [online]", December 2010. Available from: http://eur-lex.europa.eu/legal-content/EN/TXT/?uri=CELEX:52010DC0783.

portance of communication and education for European citizenship, and has done so for decades. Yet, there are huge variations across Member States in acquisition of the necessary skills for European citizenship. This is the case for example in the area of language competence although learning at least one foreign language is part of the curriculum. It is not just about courses already on offer. Is this largely a question of motivation? Language skills and citizenship are certainly made more relevant if every school child knows that at some point in his or her lifetime, they may become relevant and that Europe is also something to take to account. Thus the Council of Europe Charter on Democratic Citizenship and Human Rights' Education stresses "non-formal education" outside the formal setting and "informal education" which "means the life-long process whereby every individual acquires attitudes, values, and knowledge from the educational influences and resources in his or her environment and from daily experience." [181] Citizenship education is not therefore just about teaching in the classroom, and needs like languages, to be practised. How to offer the link between education and daily experience in the case of the more distant European context? Should mobility programmes target more those that would not otherwise have the opportunity to study abroad in the EU?

Another researcher has explained that "contrary to conventional wisdom, it is hypothesized that the impact of transnational practices on European identity is stronger among the low educated than among the highly educated."[182] This is because addressing students in higher education is "preaching to the converted" and those who already identify themselves as European. On the other hand, targeting those who leave school early, before such programmes take place, would produce far greater catch-up effects, especially since exchange programmes have already been shown to be powerful agents in forging European identity. The problem with changing policy is likely to be the lobbying factor explained in chapter 6. Higher educational institutions are well-entrenched in the current schemes and policies, whereas there is hardly any lobby for providing the European ex-

---

181 See "Charter on Education for Democratic Citizenship and Human Rights Education" available from:http://www.coe.int/en/web/edc/charter-on-education-for-democratic-citizenship-and-human-rights-education.

182 Kuhn, T. "Why Educational Exchange Programmes Miss Their Mark: Cross-Border Mobility, Education and European identify." *JCMS: Journal of Common Market Studies,* Vol. 50, pp. 994–1010, 2012.

perience as a possible second chance for the less well-educated. Should there be a right to access EU mobility programmes?

The answer should be a long-term strategy, well beyond the current financial perspectives of the European Union running from 2014-2020, to make mobility schemes a more representative reflection of European societies, whilst at the same time enlarging access to them. Since the development of the welfare state, citizenship is associated with a right of access to a range of entitlements supported through taxation. If there was a European entitlement equivalent to those associated with national citizenship, it could be "the right of every European citizen to have access to a European educational or youth exchange scheme" as suggested in the guidelines attached to this book. The European Commission might subscribe to such an objective since it originally called the "Erasmus plus" programme for 2014-2020 "Erasmus for all". The current scheme has received a 40% budget increase, which is a step in the right direction, but will only reach 4 million people. If there was a proposal to open up, step by step, the possibility for every European citizen to have access at some point in their life to such a European opportunity, how many people would actually take up such an opportunity, what would be the length of time, and what proportion of costs would be covered? It is likely that most people would be in the 20-24 age group, amounting to roughly 35 million. The cost to the taxpayer of the current programmes is roughly 3,800 euro per person. Supposing that in a given year, 19 million people decided to take up their European right, the cost would be 70 billion euro, or around half the current budget of the Union. [183] There should be a pilot project to measure interest in such an entitlement which could only be established in stages.

Should a common European citizenship card be introduced?

Apart from the limited and unequal reach of the programmes, there is also the disadvantage that they do not resemble a citizenship right, since they do not allow for direct access. The educational institution, or organisation specialised in European exchange programmes applies on behalf of the in-

---

183 An EU budget providing for an entitlement to individuals could be based on direct contributions from tax payers through a new European tax. It is sometimes argued that there should be a direct link between taxpayers and the European budget in order to strengthen a sense of being an EU citizen.

dividual. The idea of a European citizenship card is not new and is not un-controversial given the data protection risks involved. There are also the differences across Member States, some of which have mandatory ID cards, with a minority against such an option, whilst the cards themselves are either electronic incorporating modern security features or more tradi-tional.[184] There is some pressure for harmonisation of the features of cards which are used instead of passports in the Schengen area as travel docu-ments. In 1996 a high level panel on free movement of persons chaired by Simone Veil recommended the introduction of a European citizenship card, which would be optional and limited to short-term residence and emergency health care. This proposal was not taken up by the Commis-sion, which deemed that no special card was necessary for short-term resi-dence purposes. However, this has had the disadvantage that European citizens on the move face a range of very different national schemes, and a proliferation of requirements to obtain a national identification number or to register as a worker, which has created new barriers to freedom of movement.

A European citizenship card would serve a number of objectives to es-tablish rights, access and membership of the European Union:

– Providing evidence for national authorities of European rights, thus re-placing the need to supply paper originals of documents and translated certificates-a considerable reduction in "red tape" and saving of time and money for both citizens and national administrations. This would involve enlarging the scope of the European health card to cover civil status, other social rights, academic and professional qualifications.

– Allowing people to engage more easily with the European Union Insti-tutions or Member States when they apply European policy, for exam-ple to sign a citizens' initiative, a petition or put forward their views in response to a public consultation.

– Providing proof of an entitlement to access at one time of a person's choice one of the European educational, training or youth exchange programmes.

---

184 In March 2010, the Council Presidency sent out a questionnaire to EU Member States and countries that are members of the so called "Mixed Committee" that is part of Schengen (Iceland, Lichtenstein, Norway and Switzerland) to establish the "state of play concerning electronic identity cards" (Report: State of play con-cerning the electronic identity cards in the EU Member States).

Finally, the idea of such a card is a response to the need to provide European citizenship, like any citizenship, with symbols. The link with national citizenship could be made. For example, identity cards could be national on one side, and European on the other. As already pointed out in Chapter 4, European citizenship could do with a more powerful and it should be added, a more practical symbol.

(iii) Could there be a civil society movement for European citizenship?

It would seem evident that faced with questions of European rights or initiatives which touch on European policies, the individual is even more powerless than would be the case at the national level: citizens need to share their concerns if possible beyond national borders, look for support from existing civil society organisations or create new ones to carry them to the European arena and then follow up over time to keep their issues on the European agenda. When Union citizenship was introduced in the negotiations leading to the Maastricht Treaty, it was not the result of any demand coming from civil society. On the contrary, there was very little discussion of the initiative by the Spanish government either within or round the European Institutions. The debate came later and was largely national : during the process of ratification of the Maastricht Treaty and when legislation on voting rights in local and European elections was under consideration. For European civil society associations, it was the prospects of entirely other and new policies being considered for development in the Maastricht Treaty which acted as a magnet: new associations being created round public health or culture or making proposals for developing other sectoral policies further. A link between Union citizenship and these policies for a citizens' Europe was proposed by the Spanish government, but never materialised in practice. With hindsight movements in civil society, which at the time were giving far more attention to European policy making and a new Treaty linking so clearly with their particular sectoral concerns, should have given more attention to Union citizenship. This is because in the hierarchy of the Treaties and the division of competence between the Union and the Member States, Union citizenship has a more solid legal basis than the softer "citizens Europe-type" policies. We have already argued this point.

A difficulty exists however for civil society organisations to relate to citizenship. If they do so, they are likely to view it through the lens of a particular group in society whose interests they are defending or a single issue. Civil society groups are at their most effective when targeted, rather than taking on such a general theme: that would have to be the task of a broad coalition. This does not mean that European citizenship is not an issue for civil society. On the contrary most citizens' groups will claim some ownership of this first-ever transnational citizenship. The problem however is that the fragmentary way in which Union citizenship is treated by the EU Institutions reinforces the tendency for civil society to relate only to a part of the whole closest to their own concerns. For some, it is essentially about free movement rights and migration. For many, there is an issue of principle in the first place. With the introduction of Union citizenship in the Maastricht Treaty the only significant demand by civil society, particularly human rights and migrants' organisations was for its extension to legally resident third country nationals. To engage a critical mass of civil society, progress towards a more inclusive transnational citizenship would unlock the door. For others, European citizenship underpins a reform agenda for greater transparency, participation and democracy in the EU institutions. But in turn, this is a different constituency from non-governmental bodies involved with citizenship education, linguistic or cultural diversity. European citizenship therefore in the way it came from on high, and lacking a holistic framework, has ended up being pulled in different directions by civil society This matters if one believes that Union citizenship has developed over the last generation, but has reached a certain limit. The European Institutions could have done more, but given the resistance of national governments jealously guarding their sovereignty over citizenship, the next stages depend more on citizens and civil society. As the definition of citizenship at the beginning of this chapter implies, they have a duty to promote and sustain what has been achieved so far, "including the good of democratic citizenship itself". For example, a European Citizens Initiative could be the right tool to raise the need to strengthen European citizenship.[185]

---

185 ECIT is proposing a European Citizens' Initiative on full-scale, inclusive citizenship. The Commission should be invited to make proposals for a more holistic approach to European citizenship in terms of Article 25 of the Treaty on the Functioning of the European Union. To prepare the report scheduled for 2019, the Commission should carry out an opinion poll and a Europe-wide participatory process to find out what people themselves think about this first modern transnational citizenship and what they recommend for its future. The resulting recom-

To what extent is European citizenship supported by a civil society? In a haphazard and piecemeal fashion support exists but falls far short of what is needed. The obstacles to creating a civil society movement for European citizenship, which have already been referred to earlier, include:

– *Internal organisational structure.* Civil society organisations operating at European level are in general made up of national associations and do not have individual members. The extent to which, without much more developed socialisation about Europe, individual members or supporters can be truly involved is very limited. There is also the evident risk that with the requirements to become increasingly professional and match the power of the better resourced producer or commercial lobbies, public interest advocates become part of the system and lose touch with the grass roots.

– *Different national and regional contexts.* Those who share the same concerns and who could form transnational alliances are not easy to detect behind different facades whether single-issue, general purpose, lay or religious, nationally or regionally organised bodies. Their organisations reflect closely in reality, and for all their independence, the differences in state and regional structures across Europe. Most civil society organisations deal with issues which are without borders but are themselves a product of national citizenship.

---

mendations should be considered by a Convention organised by the Commission and composed of civil society activists, academics and policy makers. The scope and limits of European citizenship have to be made clear. On the one hand, it should in no way replace national citizenship. On the other hand to make European citizenship clearer and more popular its scattered pieces should be brought together as ECIT has done in the attached "Draft Guidelines on European Citizens' Rights, Involvement and Trust". Three "Es" underscore the guidelines and the demand to the Commission:

- Enforce European citizens' rights and the Charter of fundamental rights more effectively in particular to guarantee equal treatment and protection against all forms of discrimination;
- Enable the creation of infrastructure across all Member States for a European public sphere to emerge where citizen participation becomes a pillar of the EU decision-making process;
- Enlarge access to European citizenship so that everyone has an entitlement to become an Erasmus student at some point in his or her life.

This proposal can be considered as a follow-up to the European Year of citizens alliance (EYCA) which brought together the main national and European associations for the 2013 Year of citizens.

- *Diversity*. The emerging European civil society is characterised by diversity and fragmentation. These features have been intensified by the economic crisis as organisations experiment with new ways to ensure sustainability and cope with growing needs and inequality in society. More hybrid non-profit and social enterprise structures are emerging.
- *Local community development and social innovation are on the agenda*. Never before has there been so much variety across the spectrum of protest movements and innovative initiatives making full use of social media to challenge the more traditional organisations. Proposals for European citizenship could well emerge from new radical movements but are difficult to predict.
- *Mixed views about Europe*. With this shake up there is also a shake-up in attitudes over Europe, the non-profit sector being influenced by political currents whether eurosceptical or movements for European reforms and their own country's changing relationship with Europe. The weakness of the European Union in the face of repeated crises, the austerity policies and a sidelining of civil society involvement has discouraged civil society organisations in their turn from becoming involved.

It is one thing therefore to say that European citizenship needs its own civil society and another question just to locate its component parts let alone put it together. The process was helped by civil society using the European Year of citizens in 2013 to develop its own thinking about the future of Europe and European citizenship. A 25 page manifesto of the European Year of Citizens Alliance (EYCA), the 100 page citizens' pact produced by European Alternatives and much of this book are moves in a similar direction towards a more inclusive citizenship of equality. As the EYCA introduction to its policy agenda puts it: "We have been advocating for citizenship to become a transversal dimension of European policies and a key priority in all areas of the Union's action so as to move towards a truly citizen-friendly European Union that would no longer be reduced to merely economic preoccupations. For us, EU citizenship should not be confined to an individual rights-based approach but should have a strong value-based dimension so as to tackle the Europeans' sense of belonging to a common European project." [186] As pointed out in the introduction, this approach is close to the original Spanish proposals on European citizenship.

Despite the difficulties, a civil society movement for European citizenship could emerge to fill a gap. This is the only title in the Treaties for which there is no corresponding advocacy group, coalition or umbrella association of specialised European level networks. There are markedly different types of organisations involved, even among those representing European citizens directly.

– First, in the beginning, European citizens of the same nationality living in another EU Member State formed associations (beginning for example with the Italians, spreading to the Portuguese and now the Poles or Romanians). Some groups are more like cultural clubs, others more advocates for the rights of their members. Linked to such groups are foreign language media. Among the associations for populations most actively using European rights and permanently resident in another Member State, there is paradoxically less European cooperation than in many other areas of European policy. This is despite the fact that they share much in common and relate to the same regulatory framework, even though it is differently applied across Member States. From time to time such associations take their issues to the petitions committee of the European Parliament or ask the Commission to start infringement procedures against the Member State where they are resident – recognising that grouping individual complaints together with the backing of an association is the most effective way to get a European hearing.

European throughout the World (ETTW) is an example of an international associations bringing together national associations such as "Danes worldwide".

– Secondly, the sons and daughters of the first generation of European citizens appear to see civil society organisation in a different way, preferring to form clubs and associations of European citizens not of the same but of different nationalities. These are beginning to emerge in universities or major cities. For those who have been through the Erasmus experience, it appears more natural to form movements from free movement: European Alternatives, Cafe Babel, Citizens for Europe are

---

186 EYCA. *It's about Us, it's about Europe! Towards Democratic European Citizenship.* p. 1, 2013. Available from: http://euplus.org/wp-content/uploads/2015/01/the-recommendations-of-the-European-Year-of-Citizens-Alliance-2013-EYCA.pdf.

examples of this recent phenomenon. There is no doubt that this type of civil society springing directly from the practice of European citizenship and leaving one's national citizenship to one side – will grow, but the membership is low, as is the capacity to mobilise. This is evident for example in looking at a number of citizens' initiatives such as Fraternité 2020 produced by the Eurostars. One way for example to encourage debate about European citizenship would be to set up student debate circles in universities where there are significant numbers of students of different nationality, and the necessary commitment to a multi-disciplinary approach.

– Thirdly, there is a range of organisations which would consider themselves to be more "for" than "of" European citizenship, in other words the various advice and support agencies which provide information and advice or organise European exchange projects.There are distinct clusters round the three components of rights, involvement and trust in the guidelines:

Rights. Citizens' advice or law centres especially those dealing with migration issues and which have found, since EU enlargements, that their case-load of complaints from vulnerable European citizens has grown. Networking and exchanges among such groups is developing, but lacks leadership and resources. Also involved are a number of networks specifically created by the European Commission to support European citizens (ie European consumer centres or Your Europe Advice)

Involvement. There is a close network of European associations including some specialisation on issues of freedom of information, transparency, European governance, either on a full-time basis or as part of their agenda and field of activity (i.e. Statewatch, Corporate Europe Observatory or Finance Watch).

Trust. A community of interest has been developed around European experimentation with citizens' deliberations, as pointed out earlier. The process of putting together the regimes for citizens' initiatives with consultations by the Institutions has had the effect of bringing together an "ECI community" of experts and pro-democracy groups, as well as organisers of initiatives. Associations such as the European Civic Forum group have expertise in the area of non-formal citizenship education.

Civil society activists are able to point towards new ways of framing European citizenship. Despite or because of the fact the EU Institutions are locked into short term crisis management, there is a proliferation and bubbling up of civil society, citizen participatory debates about the future of Europe, particularly among the young generation. The emphasis is less on free movement of persons, a right already achieved, as on the breaking down of barriers to transnational sharing of local community development and citizen participation practices.[187]

In this chapter we are exploring the wider context of creating a European citizenship for all. Here more substantial forces could be mobilised: professionals concerned with civic education within or outside schools, the multitude of European networks which are involved with cultural, youth educational or training programmes, and a number of academic networks which have developed thinking about European citizenship from a legal, political science or sociological standpoint.[188]

The emergence of a civil society movement to support and pioneer the development of European citizenship faces substantial difficulties of diversity in approach and organisational methods. It could only take the form of a broad and inclusive coalition with European citizenship approached from many different perspectives. It depends also on further "socialisation" of European citizens. Nevertheless, as pointed out in chapter 4 on the challenges facing European citizenship, its further development depends now more on civil society than solely on the European Institutions. The start of such a process of broad coalition-building might take the form of a "summer university" of civil society activists, academics and policy makers. This is a much needed initiative but it will take time and resources to build a coalition for European citizenship.

---

187 European Alternatives is a good starting point to explore links to such movements and more radical thinking about the future of Europe and transnational active citizenship. For more information go to: https://euroalter.com/.

188 The EUDO website of the European University Institute in Florence is a good starting point for networking among academics (see: http://www.eui.eu/Projects/EUDO/Home.aspx). Also revealing is *The Development of European Identity/European Identities: Unfinished Business,* which summarises 21 projects funded by the European Commission under its research programme (see: https://ec.europa.eu/research/social-sciences/pdf/policy_reviews/development-of-european-identity-identities_en.pdf). Working document for a conference on this theme held on 9 February 2012.

CONCLUSION

This book is a response with its proposals for reform to the challenge of building a more holistic trans-national citizenship: "We must fill the gap where European citizenship is".[189] Without such a bringing together of this scattered citizenship round elements of rights, involvement and trust, it will continue to be pulled in different directions. Moreover, its development will remain uncertain even though its historical and legal foundations are more solid than generally supposed.

To meet the challenges of euroscepticism and resurgent nationalism to which it is the natural counterweight, European citizenship must be better defined. It has to move towards a perception of what ordinary people understand by citizenship where its elements are intertwined. Rights alone will not create citizenship, because people will not feel any ownership of them unless they have participated in their development. Alternatively, a citizenship of participation without rights would be dismissed as well meant but ineffective, given the practical challenges of creating a transnational public sphere. Nor are the first two really possible without a wider sense of belonging and citizenship as a status of equality. "The three components of citizenship stand or fall together."[190]

The proposal for guidelines attached to this book is consistent with the more holistic approach to Union citizenship which emerges from the analysis of the original Spanish proposals in the negotiations for the Maastricht Treaty. The European Commission is also moving in this direction with its ideas for a one-stop shop, a focal point where people can find at least a first answer to all their questions about Europe. This approach also has the advantage of avoiding the tendency of policy makers to rely on the latest isolated reform for transparency or participation only to become disappointed by the result. Single measures are never enough – a broad cross-cutting agenda alone can work. This approach should not be understood

---

189 Keating, A. "Educating Europe's citizens: moving from national to post-national models of educating for European citizenship." *Citizenship Studies,* Vol. 13, No. 2, pp. 135-151, 2009. DOI:10.1080/13621020902731140.

190 Bellamy, R. *Citizenship: A Very Short Introduction.* Oxford, Oxford University Press, 2008.

however as an attempt to create a more bureaucratic European citizenship, so much as providing a clearer understanding of what it is and what it can become. There is no reason why such a meta-framework should discourage individual specialisation and initiative. As proposed in point 24 of the guidelines a more holistic approach can well be accompanied by the development of more detailed citizen guidelines for cross-border access to goods and services or guidelines targeting particular groups in society.

The proposal to clarify European citizenship by bringing its scattered components together should not be seen either as academic or remote from people's everyday concerns about Europe. On the contrary, how can citizenship which effects different aspects of our lives be seen except as a whole? A stronger European citizenship which dares to speak its name will make the symbols of Europe a clearer affirmation of identity and popularise them. If a European team can beat the US team at golf in the Ryder cup, one day a European team might beat the Southern hemisphere at rugby or Latin America at football.

The main message is that the process of drawing up guidelines which should over time become legally binding can only have credibility if it is done by citizens themselves and accompanied by a reform agenda. Many of the reforms proposed here are not new and have either been made but need to be developed further; others have been promoted by civil society organisations and some politicians but have yet to be put on the political agenda. The advantages of approaching the reform agenda through the spectrum of a more holistic approach is that new proposals and ideas emerge. These can be summed in the following 12 point action plan:

1. A more preventative, collective and problem-solving approach to the enforcement of European rights.
2. Creation of a European free movement solidarity fund.
3. Full political rights for European citizens.
4. A more inclusive approach to European citizenship by giving access to legally resident third country nationals.
5. A better guarantee of citizens' involvement in EU policy making by making voluntary systems mandatory, user-friendly and multi-lingual.
6. Drawing up a European law for the proper conduct of citizen participation practices, including on the theme of European citizenship.
7. Easier to use citizens' initiatives, whereby over 1 million citizens can change a European law.
8. Fostering a civil society movement for European citizenship

9. Introducing a right to be informed and to education for European citizenship in schools.
10. Creating in stages an entitlement for all European citizens to participate in a European exchange programme.
11. Introducing a European citizenship card - making it easier to enforce European rights, sign European initiatives and prove such an entitlement
12. Reforming Article 25 (TFEU) so that the normal decision- making process can be used to develop European citizenship.

With a clearer understanding of what it is and an ambitious reform agenda, a more full-scale European citizenship can fulfil a role of holding a different European Union together.

Annexes

GUIDELINES
FOR EUROPEAN CITIZENS' RIGHTS,
INVOLVEMENT AND TRUST

European
Citizens' rights,
Involvement and
Trust

I. TOWARDS A FULL-SCALE EUROPEAN CITIZENSHIP

1. European citizenship is additional to and does not replace national citizenship. This first transnational citizenship of modern times is destined to become the fundamental status of the peoples of Europe built on rights, involvement and trust. European citizenship finds expression in the context of the European Union, whilst being a citizen of Europe has a geographically wider continental-scale meaning. This is a citizenship, which can only be based on shared values, rather than statehood or fixed territory and borders. It is a citizenship open to the rest of the world in a Europe, which should be a haven for refugees and asylum seekers. Where possible the same rights should be enjoyed by European citizens and all those on the territory of the European Union and neighbouring countries.

**2.** European citizenship is based on European values of democracy, human rights and the rule of law expressed in international charters, the Council of Europe Convention of Human Rights and the European Union Charter of Fundamental Rights. This places citizenship in the broader framework of traditional and modern rights to dignity, freedoms, equality, solidarity and justice.

3. A transnational citizenship is not about rights to basic services of the state, but the opening up of such services to each other on a mutual and shared basis of solidarity. To work effectively, European citizenship has its own distinct set of priority rights and concerns:

• European citizens should enjoy the freedom to move anywhere in Europe without let or hindrance caused by differences in residence rights, social security entitlements or recognition of professional and academic qualifications. Visa requirements imposed on people on the periphery of Europe should be abolished.

• To be able to move freely in Europe, citizens must have a portable right to equal treatment supported by an effective ban against discrimination based on nationality and all other forms of discrimination in all walks of life.

• Equal treatment means that special attention must be given to the most vulnerable in society. This may be because they are members of a minority such as the Roma, or because they are children, frail, elderly or suffering from a disability. It is in the nature of a European citizenship to place special emphasis on the integration of migrant workers and their families.

4. Citizens, who will receive equal attention, have the right to expect that decisions are taken as openly and as closely as possible to them. Every person has the right to have his or her affairs handled impartially, fairly and within a reasonable time by representatives of government or international organisations. This right includes:

• The right of every person to be heard before any individual measure, which would affect him or her adversely, is taken.

• The obligation of the administration to give reasons for its decisions.

5. Anyone whose rights and freedom, guaranteed by the law of the Union, become violated, has the right to an effective remedy, which includes:

• First level advice free of charge, and access to rights of appeal and effective representation.
• A fair and public hearing within a reasonable time by an independent and impartial tribunal.
• Legal aid for those who lack sufficient resources to ensure effective access to justice.
• There should be a right to appeal, provided recourse to other remedies has been exhausted, to the Council of Europe, the Court of Human Rights in Strasbourg and the European Court of Human Rights in Luxembourg.

6. European citizens benefit from rights and, therefore, responsibilities:

• To comply with each other's constitutions and laws, and uphold their shared values.
• To recognise the right of other citizens to act autonomously within the law and to take their interests into account in their own claims.
• To learn about and respect, as equal to their own, the languages and cultures of other nations.
• To act jointly in order to overcome the major challenges facing Europe and the planet which are beyond the capacity of national citizenship in small and medium-sized European states. Such challenges include: the growth of inequalities, the rise in racism and xenophobia, systematic human rights abuses, natural disasters and security threats within or outside Europe.

7. All European citizens and persons legally resident in Europe have rights:

• To be informed of their rights and the policies of elected representatives, benefiting from both freedom of information laws and the protection of their privacy.
• To be heard by public authorities before decisions are taken through easy to use consultation, deliberative and participatory mechanisms to which a measured response should be given.
• To vote, campaign and stand as candidates in all elections, whether local, regional, national or European, either in their country of residence or their country of origin, and to participate in referenda and Citizens' Initiatives.
• To petition parliaments and the executive, and present initiatives for new laws or policies signed by a minimum number of people; such initiatives should be acted upon by public institutions or be refused for good legal, budgetary or practical reasons.

II. Developing Citizenship in the Context of the European Union

A. Citizens' Rights

8. Union citizens have the right to move and reside freely within the territory of the Member States subject to the limits in the Treaties. Free movement is a fundamental right and its purpose does not need to be justified, whether it is used to work, seek work, study, train or retire. This right is extended to members of the family, spouses or recognised partners of the citizen, including those who are nationals of a third country.

This states simply that free movement is the first right of the European citizen. The limits relate to imminent threats to public order or security, and the requirements to have comprehensive sickness insurance and sufficient resources not to be a burden on the host Member State (cf. Directive 2004:38 on free movement and residence).

The aim should be to close the gap between the fine principles of European law and enforcement on the ground.

"Prevention is better than cure" and lengthy negotiations or court action to ensure that Member States comply with European directives is unhelpful. It is also important to prevent new barriers appearing.

There is a European one-stop shop with Europe Direct, Your Europe Advice and Solvit. There should be an equivalent service for citizens in each Member State, operating to European standards of service.

There is little chance that the Commission will act on an individual complaint, so group action, including in the European Court of Justice, is necessary.

9. In order to ensure the proper enforcement of European citizens' rights, the Union will adopt an action plan binding on Member States to:

• Strengthen the application of European law with preventative measures, including a requirement for Member States to notify the Commission of any draft laws or administrative practices which could lead to barriers to free movement of persons.

• Guarantee more rapid and effective access to justice by recognising that European citizens can take collective action to defend their rights including after other remedies have been exhausted in the European Court of Justice.

• Set up in each Member State a one-stop shop for information, advice and problem-solving for European citizens on the move, whilst ensuring that the same standards of service and time limits apply to European and national assistance services.

• The fund can also be used to support the integration of migrants from outside the Union. It should work in partnership with civil society organisations.

The Commission already has such power under the Treaties. The EU is considering how the Charter of Fundamental Rights can be enforced effectively.

This is a new idea. Such a fund should be based on contributions from the country of origin, the host country and the EU budget, and could be set up within EU social and regional funds.

9. (continued)

• Ensure that if a Member State has clearly violated fundamental or European citizenship rights, the Commission can file for interim measures to put an immediate stop to such practices.

• Create a European free movement solidarity fund to provide emergency help to vulnerable EU citizens and additional resources for local health, educational and housing services.

10. Citizens of the Union have the right to vote and stand as candidates in elections to the European Parliament and municipal elections in their Member State of residence. This right should be extended to national and regional elections as well as referenda.

European citizens should have full political rights and should not be deprived of the right to vote in national elections, for example, because they have exercised their right to free movement.

The Tampere Declaration of 1999 which states that: "The European Council endorses the objective that long-term legally resident third country nationals be offered the opportunity to obtain the nationality of the Member State in which they are resident."

11. All those from third countries who are legally resident in the Union should be given the opportunity to obtain the nationality of their host Member State. In this way, they become European citizens. Prior to obtaining Member State nationality, they should enjoy a set of European rights equivalent to those of European citizens.

12. European citizens have a fundamental right to the highest standards of protection of their personal data. Given the expansion of the internet and data available to commercial enterprises and public authorities, the European Union will adopt laws to ensure that protection of privacy keeps in step with technological progress.

Article 8 of the Charter of Fundamental Rights gives a higher priority to data protection.

B. Involvement

This article is based on Article 24 TFEU which refers to the right to petition the European Ombudsman.

However there is a deliberate extension to Article 24 TFEU envisaged here. In particular, we propose extending these rights to (non-citizen) residents of the Member States.

This second bullet point seeks to strengthen the accountability of the Commission towards complainants.

This article also seeks to fill a gap between a normal petition, which can be signed by a single individual, and a Citizens' Initiative with the collection of one million signatures.

A number of points of access for citizens to the EU exist, free of charge. In some cases, not in all, time limits exist for answering citizens' appeals or handling complaints. Legislation should be introduced or revised to provide for more uniform standards.

13. Citizens of the Union and any natural or legal person residing or having their office in a Member State have the right to:

• Write to any of the Institutions, agencies and bodies of the Union in one of the official languages and receive an answer within a reasonable time in the same language.

• Submit an individual or collective complaint of a violation of European law or rights and be informed of the action taken.

• To be heard by the competent European Parliament committee if their petition receives more than 100,000 signatures from a minimum of 7 Member States.

• Make a complaint regarding an instance of maladministration by the Union authorities to the European Ombudsman or, where individual interests are directly affected, to the European Court of Justice.

• Receive diplomatic and consular protection from any Member State, in a third country in which their state or country of residence is not represented.

The European Union will adopt a law to establish time limits for response to citizens' complaints or requests and other standards of good administrative practice for all EU Institutions and agencies. These time limits and standards will also apply to Member States' administrations and agencies when dealing with European citizens.

14. Freedom of information is essential to the practice of EU citizenship. Any citizen of the Union and any natural or legal person residing or established in a Member State will have the right to access documents subject to the limits established, whatever their medium, from the Union's Institutions and agencies, and in particular:

• To know the position of their government in EU negotiations.

• To access all documents of a legislative nature or which could lead to legislation.

• To access documents relating to international agreements or treaties which have an impact on European standards.

Each Institution and agency will appoint an independent information commissioner to assist citizens in their search for documents.

Like the proposal above on data protection the aim is to give more prominence to the right. It builds on and strengthens Article 15 TFEU and Article 12 of the Charter of Fundamental Rights.

"Subject to the limits established" refers to the mandatory and optional exemptions in the regulation 1049/2001 on access to documents. For example, there is a need for more transparency in the EU-US negotiations for a Transatlantic Trade and Investment Partnership (TTIP) according to the European Ombudsman.

Transparency of the legislative and decision-making process can be achieved if transparency is applied not only to the EU Institutions, but also to lobbying practices.

The current voluntary register of organised interests is incomplete and entries often inaccurate, giving citizens only a general idea of the extent of lobbying practices which have expanded in recent years. There are at least 30,000 lobbyists round the EU Institutions.

In his speech to the European Parliament on 15 July 2014, the incoming Commission President, Jean-Claude Juncker promised to make the transparency register legally binding and extend it from the Commission and European Parliament to the Council of Ministers.

15. European citizens have a right to know which organisations, whether public or private are making representations to the EU Institutions on which specific issues and with what resources. In this way, they are able to judge whether the process is fair and balanced. A European law should:

• Make inclusion on the transparency register mandatory for all organisations seeking to influence the European Institutions.

• Ensure that entries are accurate, complete and up to date by regular checks and appropriate sanctions for non-compliance.

• Provide for the register to cover all Institutions, bodies and agencies of the EU.

16. European citizens have a right to be heard by the Institutions. Public consultations are a means to reach the majority of citizens' interests and ensure the widest possible input to decision-making. The Commission's standards for consultation should become mandatory and apply to the other Institutions and to Member States when they develop their responses to European initiatives. In particular:

• Consultations should be widely advertised in a more friendly way in particular to engage with minority interests and hard-to-reach groups.

• The aims and questions should be formulated to be accessible to lay persons and available in all official languages.

• There should be appropriate feedback and explanation as to why certain views expressed were accepted and others rejected.

> Consultation standards should be mandatory, widely used, multilingual, accessible, and a means of dialogue with citizens. In terms of Article 11 of the Treaty on the European Union, the standards should apply not only to the Commission when it initiates a draft legislation but to the other Institutions and Members States.

C. Trust

> A right to be informed was first proposed when the Commission on the Future of Europe was considering the draft Constitutional Treaty. The proposal was supported by the Commission and European Parliament at the time, but has yet to be included on the agenda for Treaty reform.

17. All citizens of the Union, and all natural persons residing in a Member State, shall be informed about their European rights and activities of the European Union, so as to be better able to participate in European policy making. The Union Institutions and Member States will:

• Listen to citizens

• Produce factual and objective information about European Union activities, expressed in clear and understandable language.

• Provide and disseminate this information by all available means in a socially balanced way in all official languages.

• Give every European citizen of voting age a handbook about European rights and how to find out more about the European Union. Also see point 22 on education about European citizenship.

18. Participatory and deliberative processes should become a pillar of the European Union's decision-making, so as to give citizens an effective voice both in setting priorities and ways to improve the quality and enforcement of legislation. A European law should be adapted to ensure that there is regular use of such practices and that they meet fair and democratic standards. Such practices should be applied across all Member States with a representative sample of the population proposing how to develop European citizenship itself.

> Plan D for democracy, dialogue and debate showed that such processes as citizens' consultations, juries or town hall meetings can work at European level. They should become more systematic and conform to standards.
>
> Such standards relate to representative recruitment of citizens, access to expertise and engagement with decision-makers and information on the results.

19. European Citizens' Initiatives (ECIs) for which over 1 million signatures are required from a minimum of 7 Member States should be easier to use. The EU Institutions should:

• Make the temporary provision to ECI organisers of a secure server for online signature collection permanent

• Simplify and harmonise the requirement for signature collection across Member States, name and address being sufficient.

• Encourage the setting up of an independent European fund to which applications can be made for start-up grants, and reimbursement of a share of the costs for successful ECIs.

• Allow all European citizens and legally resident third country nationals to sign an initiative from the age of sixteen.

In light of the experience with the first three years of ECIs and the high failure rate, reforms are essential to make the regime simpler and more uniform. Revision is scheduled for 2015.

For ECIs to become a genuine citizens' right, and avoid its capture by lobbyists and powerful interests, such financial support is necessary.

Access to this first ever transnational agenda setting instrument should be as wide as possible.

This article is based on Article 14 TEU whilst supporting reforms to make the European elections more European. This can be achieved through more competition among candidates for Commission President and other high office functions as well as taking a step towards a European constituency. The Parliament could also at least study the issue of EU-wide referenda.

20. The European Parliament, elected by direct universal suffrage, represents European citizens and is the main advocate of their concerns in the decision-making of the Union. In particular:

• Each European political party should put forward its candidate for President of the European Commission to give voters choice.

• Citizens should have the choice also of voting for candidates on transnational party lists, to enhance the European character of the elections.

• The European Parliament should propose how EU-wide referenda could be introduced to allow citizens to choose vital options for Europe's future.

This is close to the writing of Article 11 (TEU), which calls for the creation of a European public space. The rest of this article relates to long-standing demands for the "Europeanisation" of civil society, which is essential to the development of European citizenship.

22. A full-scale European citizenship cannot be achieved without education. All European citizens have a right from a young age to education about European citizenship. After widespread consultations, the Commission will propose:

• A model teaching manual in all languages for use in schools and out-of-school activity.

• Recommendations to Member States to add a European dimension to their own programmes for citizenship education, in particular when it is related to the teaching of history and languages.

A right to be informed and educated for European citizenship does not mean much if there appears to be little chance to put it into practice. A universal entitlement may have some support in the Commission which first called its new programmes "Erasmus for all" and some support among Member States which increased the budget by 40% for 2014-2020. However, such an entitlement will only be phased in gradually in conjunction with a European citizenship card.

21. In order to develop European citizenship as a way to connect different languages and cultures, the European Institutions will in terms of Article 11 (TEU):

• Provide citizens with their own European public space to exchange views on all areas of transnational action. The Institutions should make available e-participation tools and facilities for face-to-face dialogue.

• Encourage citizens to play their part in the building of Europe through the adoption of a European association statute and a pact for open dialogue between the European Institutions and civil society.

• Further develop the programmes for transnational exchange of best practices and projects in the areas of culture, consumer, environmental, health, social protection and territorial cohesion policies which are closely linked to European citizenship.

The competence of the European Commission is limited when it comes to education, but it does have competence to recommend European citizenship to be added as a theme to national civic education.

23. All European citizens should be given on an equal basis, a once-in-a-lifetime opportunity to participate in a European educational training or youth programme in another European country. The European Commission should propose:

• How to develop such an entitlement on the basis of the Union's Erasmus plan and life-long learning programmes.

• The conditions attached to such an entitlement and the timetable for putting the necessary resources in place.

• A European citizenship card both as a symbol and proof of such an entitlement, other European rights and a means of signing Citizens' Initiatives, and petitioning and voting in the European elections.

THE A-Z FOR THE ASTUTE CITIZEN

A - Access to documents:
As established in Article 15 TFEU, every citizen and resident of the Member States has the right to access to documents of EU institutions. For more information:
http://ec.europa.eu/transparency/access_documents/index_en.htm

B - Budget and EU funding for citizen projects:
Europe for Citizens is a programme divided in two strands: "Remembrance and European citizenship" and "Democratic engagement and civic participation". For more information:
https://eacea.ec.europa.eu/europe-for-citizens_en
http://www.ecas.org/resource-centre/eu-funding-advice/

C - Citizens Initiative
Under Regulation no 211/2011, a legislative proposal can be submitted to the European Commission as long as it is signed by at least 1 million citizens from seven different Member States. For more information:
http://ec.europa.eu/citizens-initiative/public/welcome?lg=en

D – Directive on European citizenship
A European Directive sets an objective and allows each Member State to implement through national laws. The so-called citizenship Directive (2004/38) introduced a set of free movement rights for every European citizen and their families. For more information:
http://eur-lex.europa.eu/LexUriServ/LexUriServ.do?uri=OJ:L:2004:158:0
077:0123:en:PDF

E – Erasmus +
This programme creates more opportunities for students to study abroad in Europe. In addition to this, the EU offers lifelong learning programmes. For more information
http://ec.europa.eu/programmes/erasmus-plus/index_en.htm

F – Free movement of people in the European Union
One of the basic rights conferred to European citizens. For more information:
http://ec.europa.eu/justice/citizen/move-live/index_en.htm

G – Green paper
A Green Paper is a document issued by the Commission aiming to fostering debate and consultation among relevant actors and citizens on a specific topic. Find an index:
http://ec.europa.eu/green-papers/index_en.htm

H – Human rights
The European Court of Human Rights (ECHR) is based in Strasbourg, and
The European Court of Justice (ECJ) is based in Luxemburg. The first acts
as the guardian of the European Convention of Human Rights and the second of the Charter of Fundamental Rights of the EU. For more information:
http://www.echr.coe.int/Pages/home.aspx?p=home&c=
http://europa.eu/about-eu/institutions-bodies/court-justice/index_en.htm

I – Institutions of the European Union and how they work
You can find this information at one of the 800 information points near
you:
http://europa.eu/index_en.htm

J – Justice
DG Justice has a specific department for European citizenship. For more
information:
http://ec.europa.eu/justice/citizen/index_en.htm

K – Karlsruhe Court
The ruling on the Lisbon Treaty by the German Constitutional Court is
highly significant since it denied the existence of a European *demos* and a
truly European public sphere. More information below:
http://www.institutdelors.eu/media/karlsruheeuropeauel-baquerocruznejul
y10.pdf?pdf=ok

L – Lisbon Treaty
This Treaty aims to achieve "a more democratic and transparent Europe" and "a Europe of rights and values, freedom, solidarity and security''. For more information:
http://eur-lex.europa.eu/legal-content/EN/TXT/?uri=CELEX:12012E/TXT

M –Maastricht Treaty
This treaty stands as a milestone of the EU, with the creation of the concept of European citizenship. For more information:
http://europa.eu/eu-law/decision-making/treaties/pdf/treaty_on_european_union/treaty_on_european_union_en.pdf

N - NGOs – Civil society
An involved civil society has a key role to play in European citizenship. To see what has been done:
http://ec.europa.eu/citizenship/index_en.htm
http://www.citizensforeurope.eu/
http://euplus.org/wp-content/uploads/2015/01/the-recommendations-of-the-European-Year-of-Citizens-Alliance-2013-EYCA.pdf
http://www.civic-forum.eu/

O - European Ombudsman
This independent body investigates complaints coming from citizens regarding possible maladministration in EU institutions, agencies or bodies. For more information:
http://www.ombudsman.europa.eu/en/

P – Petitions to European Parliament
Thanks to Article 227 TFEU any European citizen can issue a complaint or observation regarding the application of EU law or demand of the European Parliament to adopt a position on a specific subject. For further information:
http://www.europarl.europa.eu/atyourservice/en/20150201PVL00037/Petitions
http://www.europarl.europa.eu/sides/getDoc.do?pubRef=-//EP//NONSGML+REPORT+A7-2014-0131+0+DOC+PDF+V0//EN

Q – Quo Vadis Europe
A vast amount of academic research is dedicated to the future of the European Union. Find more information in:
http://www.eu.thinktankdirectory.org/
http://www.epin.org/new/home
http://www.ceps.be/
http://www.euroalter.com/

R- Regulation
A European regulation is a binding legislative act, applied in the whole European Union. Regulation No 883/2004 established a coordination of social security systems. Find more information here:
http://eur-lex.europa.eu/legal-content/EN/TXT/PDF/?uri=CELEX:02004R0883-20130108

S – Subsidiarity
This principle establishes that the Union does not take action unless it is in areas that are its exclusive competence or it if its action is more effective than if taken at a lower level. More information in:
https://europadatenbank.iaaeu.de/user/view_legalact.php?id=63

T – Transparency register
It lists which interests that are being represented at the European level. They have to declare how much they spend in lobbying and its activities. The Commission has promised that registering will be mandatory soon. Find more information here:
http://ec.europa.eu/transparencyregister/public/homePage.do?redir=false&locale=en

U – Universities
European citizenship is an increasingly researched topic throughout European universities. Find more information in:
http://eudo-citizenship.eu/eu-citizenship
http://www.beucitizen.eu
https://macimide.maastrichtuniversity.nl/

V – Volunteering
The European Voluntary Service programme supports people who want to volunteer up to a year in another European country. Find out more about this in:
http://ec.europa.eu/youth/programme/mobility/european-voluntary-service _en.htm

W – White paper
Documents that announce action by the Commission in a specific area. More recently, important policy initiatives are announced in "communications". See an index below:
http://ec.europa.eu/white-papers/index_en.htm

X – Xenophobia (fight against)
The Amsterdam Treaty set the legal basis for combating discrimination of any kind. After 2000, the Council approved several directives and programmes were created to prevent discrimination. For more information:
http://eur-lex.europa.eu/legal-content/EN/TXT/?qid=1432576190875&uri =CELEX:11997E013
http://ec.europa.eu/social/main.jsp?langId=en&catId=327

Y – European Year of citizens
The European Union promotes different issues by proclaiming an "official year". 2013 was "year of citizens". The list with all years below:
http://europa.eu/citizens-2013/about/

Z – Zambrano and other relevant cases

There is a vast number of cases that deal with the enforcement of European citizens' rights. The cases Van Gend en Loos, Martínez Sala, Baumbast, Zambrano, Metock, Chen and Dano, or stand among others. For more information:

http://eur-lex.europa.eu/legal-content/EN/ALL/?uri=CELEX:61962CJ0026

http://eur-lex.europa.eu/legal-content/EN/TXT/?qid=1432577662408&uri=CELEX:61996CJ0085

http://eur-lex.europa.eu/legal-content/EN/TXT/?qid=1432578275319&uri=CELEX:C2002/274/03

http://eur-lex.europa.eu/legal-content/EN/TXT/?qid=1432577699567&uri=CELEX:62009CJ0034

http://eur-lex.europa.eu/legal-content/EN/TXT/?qid=1432578347971&uri=CELEX:62008CJ0127

http://eur-lex.europa.eu/legal-content/EN/TXT/?qid=1432578380813&uri=CELEX:62002CJ0200

http://eur-lex.europa.eu/legal-content/EN/TXT/?qid=1432578225531&uri=CELEX:62013CJ0333

BIBLIOGRAPHY

Anglmayer, I. *Implementation of the European Citizens' Initiative: The experience of the first three years.* European Parliamentary Research Service: Brussels, 2015.

Arauzo, E., Hoedeman, O., Tansey, R. *Rescue the Register! How to make EU lobby transparency credible and reliable* [online]. Alliance for Lobbying Transparency and Ethics Regulation (ALTER-EU), June 2013. Available from: http://www.alter-e u.org/sites/default/files/documents/Rescue_the_Register_report_25June2013.pdf .

Barca, F. *An agenda for reformed cohesion policy: A place-based approach to meeting European Union challenges and expectations* [online], 2009. Available from: http:// ec.europa.eu/regional_policy/archive/policy/future/pdf/report_barca_v 0306.pdf.

Bellamy, R. 'The liberty of the moderns: Market freedom and democracy within the EU.' *Global Constitutionalism,* Vol. 1, No. 1, pp. 141-172, 2012. DOI: 10.1017/ S2045381711000086.

Bellamy, R. *Citizenship: A Very Short Introduction.* Oxford, Oxford University Press, 2008.

Bellamy, R., Castiglione, D., Shaw, J. (eds.) *Making European Citizens: Civic Inclusion in a Transnational Context.* Basingstoke, Palgrave Macmillan, 2006.

Bellamy, R., Castiglione D., and Shaw, J. (eds.) "Introduction: From National to Transnational Citizenship' in *Making European Citizens: Civic Inclusion in a Transnational Context.* Basingstoke: Palgrave Macmillan, pp. 1-31, 2006.

Belot, M., Ederveen, S. "Cultural and institutional barriers in migration between OECD countries", Mimeo, 2006.

Berg, J., Freund, D. "Legislative footprint: What's the real influence of lobbying? [online]", Transparency International EU Office, 2015. Available from: http://www.tra nsparencyinternational.eu/wp-content/uploads/2015/03/The-EU-Legislative-Footpri nt.pdf.

Bertsou, E. The 2014 European Parliament elections: A victory for European Democracy. LSE "Europe in question" Discussion paper series, 2014.

Besson, S., Utzinger, A. "Introduction: Future Challenges of European Citizenship – Facing a Wide-Open Pandora's Box." *European Law Journal,* Vol. 13, No. 5, pp. 573-590, September 2007.

BEUCITIZEN. "Social rights of EU migrant citizens: A comparative perspective", 2015. Available from: http://beucitizen.eu/wp-content/uploads/Deliverable-6.1_fina ll.pdf.

Carrera S. 'The Framing of the Roma as Abnormal EU Citizens: Assessing European Politics on Roma Evictions and Expulsions in France' in: E. Guild (ed.) *The Reconceptualization of European Union Citizenship*, pp. 33–63. Leiden: Brill Nijhoff, 2014.

Dhéret, C., Lazarowicz, A., Nicoli, F., Pascouau, Y., Zuleeg, F. *Making progress towards the completion of the single European labour market* [online]. EPC Issue Paper no. 75, European Policy Centre, May 2013. Available from: http://www.epc.eu/documents/uploads/pub_3529_single_european_labour_market.pdf.

Duff, A. *Post-national democracy and the reform of the European Parliament* [online], Policy Paper No. 42, October 2010. Available from: www.notre-europe.eu.

European Commision. "COM(2015)671 final of 15.12.2015 on the European Border and Coast Guard [online]." Available from: http://ec.europa.eu/dgs/home-affairs/wh at-we-do/policies/securing-eu-borders/legal documents/docs/regulation_on_the_eur opean_border_and_coast_guard_en.pdf

European Commission. "Communication from the Commission to the European Parliament, the Council, the European Economic and Social Committee and the Committee of Regions: Better regulation for better results – An EU agenda [online]." COM(2015), Strasbourg 19.5.2015. Available from: http://ec.europa.eu/smart-regul ation/better_regulation/documents/com_2015_215_en.pdf.

European Commission. "Report from the Commission on the application in 2014 of Regulation (EC) No 1049/2001 regarding public access to European Parliament, Council and Commission documents [online]." COM(2014) 619, 2014. Available from: http://ec.europa.eu/transparency/access_documents/docs/rapport_2013/com-2 014-619_en.pdf.

European Commission. *EU Citizenship Report 2013* [online]. 2013. Available from: http://ec.europa.eu/justice/citizen/files/2013eucitizenshipreport_en.pdf.

European Commission. "COM/2013/0837 final. Free movement of EU citizens: Five actions to make a difference [online]." Available from: http://eur-lex.europa.eu/lega l-content/en/ALL/?uri=celex%3A52013DC0837.

European Commission. "Commission report on the application of Directive 2003/109/EC concerning the status of third country nationals who are long-term residents (COM (2011)585 final) of 28.9.2011 [online]." 2011. Available from: http://ec.europa.eu/dgs/home-affairs/what-we-do/policies/pdf/1_en_act_part1_v 62_ en.pdf.

European Commission. *New Europeans.* Special Eurobarometer [online]. April 2011. Available from: http://ec.europa.eu/public_opinion/archives/ebs/ebs_346_en.pdf.

European Commission. "The memory of crimes committed by totalitarian regimes in Europe (COM(2010) 788 final of 22.12.2010 [online]." December 2010. Available from: http://eur-lex.europa.eu/legal-content/EN/TXT/?uri=CELEX:52010DC0783.

European Commission, Institute for Human Science, Biedenkopf, K., Geremek, B., Michalski, K. *The Spiritual and Cultural Dimension of Europe* [online], Vienna/ Brussels, October 2004. Available from: ftp://ftp.cordis.europa.eu/pub/citizens/docs /citizens_michalski_091104_report_annexes_en.pdf.

European Commission. "COM/2001/0506 final. Third Report from the Commission on Citizenship of the Union [online]", 2001. Available from: http://eur-lex.europa.eu/le galcontent/EN/TXT/?uri=CELEX:52001DC0506.

European Council. *Council Annual Report on Access to Documents 2013.* 2013.

European Council. "Regulation (EEC) No 1612/68 of the Council of 15 October 1968 on freedom of movement for workers within the Community online]", 1968. Available from: http://eur-lex.europa.eu/legal-content/en/TXT/?uri=celex%3A31968R16 12.

European Ombudsman. *Annual Report 2014* [online]. 2014. Available from: http://ww w.ombudsman.europa.eu/en/activities/annualreport.faces/en/59959/html.bookmark.

European Parliament. "2013 Annual Report of the European Parliament on Public Access to Documents (Regulation (EC) No 1049/2001 – Article 17 [online]." 2013. Available from: http://www.europarl.europa.eu/register/pdf/rapport_annuel_2013_ EN.pdf.

Eurydice. *Citizenship Education in Europe* [online]. Brussels, Education, Audiovisual and Culture Executive Agency, 2012. Available from: http://eacea.ec.europa.eu/edu cation/eurydice/.

EYCA. *It's about Us, it's about Europe! Towards Democratic European Citizenship* [online]. p. 1, 2013. Available from: http://euplus.org/wp-content/uploads/2015/01/t he-recommendations-of-the-European-Year-of-Citizens-Alliance-2013-EYCA.pdf.

Frevert, U. 'How to become a good European citizen: present challenges and past experiences.' in Georgi, V. B. (ed.) *The Making of Citizens in Europe: New Perspectives on Citizenship Education,* pp. 37-51, Bonn: Bundeszentrale fur politische Bildung, 2008.

Georgi, V. B. (ed.) *The Making of Citizens in Europe: New Perspectives on Citizenship Education.* Bonn: Bundeszentrale fur politische Bildung, 2008.

Goudappel, F. *The Effects of EU Citizenship: Economic, Social and Political Rights in a Time of Constitutional Change.* The Hague: TMC Asser Press, 2010.

Greenwood, J., Drezer, J. "The Transparency register: A European vanguard of strong lobby regulation?" *Interest Groups & Advocacy*, Vol. 2, pp. 139–162, April 2013. DOI:10.1057/iga.2013.3.

Guild, E. *The European Union after the Treaty of Lisbon: Fundamental Rights and the EU citizenship* [online]. CEPS Liberty and Security in Europe/June 2010, Global Jean Monnet/European Community Studies Association, 2010. Available from: http://aei.pitt.edu/15107/1/Guild_Jean_Monnet_speech_e-version.pdf.

Habermas, J. *The Crisis of the European Union: A Response.* Cambridge: Polity Press, 2012.

Held, D. *Models of Democracy.* 3rd ed. Cambridge: Polity Press, 2006.

Heremans, T. *Public access to documents: Jurisprudence between principle and practice (between jurisprudence and recast.* Egmont Paper no. 50, Brussels: Academia Press for Egmont - The Royal Institute for International Relations, September 2011.

Hillebrandt, Z. M., Curtin, D., Meijer, A. "Transparency in the EU Council of Ministers: An Institutional Analysis." *European Law Journal,* Vol. 20, No. 1, pp. 1-20, January 2012. DOI: 10.1111/eulj.12051.

Hix, S. *What's Wrong With the European Union and How to Fix It.* Oxford: Polity Press, 2008.

Jacobs, F. G. "Citizenship of the European Union - A Legal Analysis." *European Law* Journal, 13(5), pp. 591-610, September 2007.

Kaldor, M., Selchow, S. ,Deel, S., Murray-Leach, T. *The 'bubbling up' of subterranean politics in Europe.* Civil Society and Human Security Research Unit, London School of Economics and Political Science, London, UK, 2012.

Keating, A. "Educating Europe's citizens: moving from national to post-national models of educating for European citizenship." *Citizenship Studies,* Vol. 13, No. 2, pp. 135-151, 2009. DOI:10.1080/13621020902731140.

Kritzinger, S. "European Identity Building from the Perspective of Efficiency." *Comparative European Politics,* Vol. 3, pp. 50-75, 2005.

Kuhn, T. "Why Educational Exchange Programmes Miss Their Mark: Cross-Border Mobility, Education and European identify." *JCMS: Journal of Common Market Studies,* Vol. 50, pp. 994–1010, 2012.

Maas, W. 'The Evolution of EU Citizenship' in *Making History: European Integration and Institutional Change at Fifty. The State of the European Union, Vol. 8.* ed by Meunier, S., McNamara, K. R., Oxford: Oxford University Press, pp. 231-247, 2007.

Maas, W. *Challenges of European Citizenship.* Paper presented at the annual meeting of the American Political Science Association, Philadelhia PA, 1 September 2006.

Maas, W. "The Genesis of European Rights". *JCMS: Journal of Common Market Studies*, Vol. 43, No. 5, pp.1009-1025, 2005.

Maslowski, S. "The Expulsion of European Union Citizens from the Host Member State: Legal Grounds and Practice" *Central and Eastern European Migration Review* [online]. Available from: http://www.ceemr.uw.edu.pl/vol-4-no-2-december-2 015/articles/expulsion-european-union-citizens-host-member-state-legal-grounds.

McNamara, K. The Politics of everyday Europe: Constructing Authority in the European Union. Oxford: Oxford University Press, 2015.

Moro, G. (ed.) *The Single Currency and European Citizenship: Unveiling the Other Side of the Coin.* New York: Bloomsbury, 2013.

Pateman, C. 'Participatory Democracy Revisited.' *Perspective on Politics*, Vol. 10, No. 1, pp. 7-19, March 2012. DOI: 10.1017/S1537592711004877.

Perez-Diaz, V. cited in Warleigh, A. 'Making Citizens from the Market? NGOs and the Representation of Interests' in Bellamy, R., Castiglione, D., Shaw, J. (eds) Making European Citizens: Civic Inclusion in a Transnational Context. Basingstoke: Palgrave Macmillan, pp. 118-133, 2006.

Piris, J. C. *The Future of Europe: Towards a Two-Speed EU?* Cambridge: Cambridge University Press.

Rasmussen, M. K. *Lobbying* the *European Parliament*: *A Necessary Evil*. CEPS Policy Brief No. 242. May 10, 2005.

Recchi, E. et al. *The Europeanisation of Everyday Life: Cross-Border Practices and Transnational Identities among EU and Third-Country Citizens. Final Report* [online] . EUCROSS, June 2014. Available from:http://www.eucross.eu/cms/index.php ?option=com_content&view=article&id=8:the-eucross-project&catid=14:home&Ite mid=160.

Recchi, E., Favell, A. (eds.) *Pioneers of European Integration: Citizenship and Mobility in the EU.* Cheltenham: Edward Elgar Publishing Ltd., 2009.

Riso, S. S., Olivier, J. E., Andersen, T. *Labour migration in the EU: Recent trends and policies.* Eurofound, Publications Office of the European Union: Luxembourg, 2014. Also available online from: http://www.eurofound.europa.eu/publications/rep ort/2014/eu-member-states/labour-market-social-policies/labour-mobility-in-the-eu-recent-trends-and-policies.

Schmitt, H., Hobolt, S, B., Popa, S. A. "Does personalization increase turnout? Spitzenkandidaten in the 2014 European Parliament elections" *European Union Politics*, pp. 1-22, 2015.

Shaw, J. *Citizenship: Contrasting Dynamics at the Interface of Integration and Constitutionalism.* European University Institute (EUI) Working Paper RSCAS 2010/60. San Domenico Di Fiesole, EUI, 2010.

Sintomer, Y., Herberg, C., Roecke, A. "Participatory Budgeting in Europe: Potentials and Challenges", *International Journal of Urban and Regional Research*, Vol. 31, No. 1, pp. 164–78, 2008, DOI:10.1111/j.1468-2427.2008.00777.x

Tansey, R., Cann, V. *New and Improved? Why the EU Lobby register still fails to deliver* [online]. Alliance for Lobbying Transparency and Ethics Regulation (ALTER-EU), January 2015. Available from: http://alter-eu.org/documents/2015/01.

Téglas, P. *"The European Citizens' Initiative – (Un)successful Tool of Deliberative Democracy; Present State and Future Perspectives [online]"*, *2015. Available from:* http://ecit-foundation.eu/.

Tindemans, L. "European Union: Report by Mr Leo Tindemans, Prime Minister of Belgium to the European Council." *Bulletin of the European Communities,* 1/76, 1975.

Warleigh, A. 'Making Citizens from the Market? NGOs and the Representation of Interests.' in *Making European Citizens: Civic Inclusion in a Transnational Context.* ed. by Bellamy, R., Castiglione, D., Shaw, J. Basingstoke: Palgrave Macmillan: pp. 118-133, 2006.

Van Eijken, H. *European Citizenship and the Constitutionalisation of the European Union.* Utrecht, Utrecht University, 2014.

Van Oorshot, W. 'Making the difference in social Europe: deservingness perceptions among citizens of European welfare states', *Journal of European Social Policy*, Vol. 16, No. 1, pp. 23-42, 2006.

van Schendelen, R. *The Art of Lobbying the EU: More Machiavelli in Brussels.* 4th ed. Amsterdam: Amsterdam University Press, 2013.